W9-CUH-647

ACCESS 2
FOR
DUMMIES™

Quick Reference

by Stuart J. Stuple

IDG BOOKS

IDG Books Worldwide, Inc.
An International Data Group Company

San Mateo, California ♦ Indianapolis, Indiana ♦ Boston, Massachusetts

Access 2 For Dummies Quick Reference

Published by
IDG Books Worldwide, Inc.
An International Data Group Company
155 Bovet Road, Suite 310
San Mateo, CA 94402

Library of Congress Catalog Card No.: 94-75723

ISBN: 1-56884-167-1

Printed in the United States of America

10 9 8 7 6 5 4 3 2 1

1C/QU/QV/ZU

Distributed in the United States by IDG Books Worldwide, Inc.

Distributed in Canada by Macmillan of Canada, a Division of Canada
Publishing Corporation; by Computer and Technical Books in Miami, Florida,
for South America and the Caribbean; by Longman Singapore in Singapore,
Malaysia, Thailand, and Korea; by Toppan Co. Ltd. in Japan; by Asia
Computerworld in Hong Kong; by Woodslane Pty. Ltd. in Australia and New
Zealand; and by Transword Publishers Ltd. in the U.K. and Europe.

For information on where to purchase IDG Books outside the U.S., contact
Christina Turner at 415-312-0633.

For information on translations, contact Marc Jeffrey Mikulich, Foreign Rights
Manager, at IDG Books Worldwide; FAX NUMBER 415-358-1260.

For sales inquiries and special prices for bulk quantities, write to the address
above or call IDG Books Worldwide at 415-312-0650.

 is a trademark of IDG Books Worldwide, Inc.

Acknowledgments

To start, I want to thank those who provided that special, personal effort: Bjoern for putting up with it all; the pet patrol — Astral for sleeping on the keyboard even though it must be uncomfortable and the dogs, Heida and Idunna, for exempting the Access documentation from the chewing campaign; and Devra for being there when I called for help in converting a hundred files from BMP to PCX. I also want to thank all of my friends for their support, especially greater metropolitan Woodbridge, the (funny) business division at Glendale, and the "country folk" of Seattle.

I also want to thank all of the people at IDG who made this book possible. That includes the bosses: John Kilcullen for remembering my name and offering his encouragement and David Solomon for whatever it is he does in that spacious office. A special thanks to Janna Custer who came through with this project so that I could make my rent and Megg Bonar who made sure that I actually got my check. Then there's the editorial crew. Starting at the top, thanks to Mary Bednarek for so many things (but especially polenta and crabcakes). For making this book readable, thanks to Diane Steele who got me started and then passed me to Laurie Smith who managed to return all my annoying phone calls and passed me to Tim Gallan who actually translated my writing into English. Then there's Michael Partington who served as technical editor — thanks for not recommending that I try fiction next time. Finally, a special thanks to a few members of the IDG production team: Beth Baker, who runs the show, and Sherry Gomoll (even though she only had to lay this book out once), who placed over 250 little tiny pictures of Access buttons. And Sharon Hilgenberg who did the index so that you could find things easier deserves a special thanks.

The publisher would like to give special thanks to Patrick J. McGovern, without whom this book would not have been possible.

About the Author

Stuart J. Stuple has worked with computers since before personal computing was a reality. He got his start on a series of DEC machines running Unix, but now leads a very balanced existence — his desk has both a Macintosh and a Windows machine. In addition to work for other publishers, he was a contributor to the *PC World Dos 6 Handbook* (by IDG Books) and has worked in various capacities on over a dozen other IDG titles. He has a Masters degree in Counseling Psychology and has been a member of the faculty at community colleges in both California and Washington. He currently works as a freelance editor and author, mostly so that he can play with new software.

About IDG Books Worldwide

Welcome to the world of IDG Books Worldwide.

IDG Books Worldwide, Inc., is a division of International Data Group, the world's largest publisher of computer-related information and the leading global provider of information services on information technology. IDG publishes over 194 computer publications in 62 countries. Forty million people read one or more IDG publications each month.

If you use personal computers, IDG Books is committed to publishing quality books that meet your needs. We rely on our extensive network of publications, including such leading periodicals as *Macworld, InfoWorld, PC World, Publish, Computerworld, Network World*, and *SunWorld*, to help us make informed and timely decisions in creating useful computer books that meet your needs.

Every IDG book strives to bring extra value and skill-building instruction to the reader. Our books are written by experts, with the backing of IDG periodicals, and with careful thought devoted to issues such as audience, interior design, use of icons, and illustrations. Our editorial staff is a careful mix of high-tech journalists and experienced book people. Our close contact with the makers of computer products helps ensure accuracy and thorough coverage. Our heavy use of personal computers at every step in production means we can deliver books in the most timely manner.

We are delivering books of high quality at competitive prices on topics customers want. At IDG, we believe in quality, and we have been delivering quality for over 25 years. You'll find no better book on a subject than an IDG book.

John Kilcullen
President and C.E.O.
IDG Books Worldwide, Inc.

IDG Books Worldwide, Inc. is a division of International Data Group. The officers are Patrick J. McGovern, Founder and Board Chairman; Walter Boyd, President. International Data Group's publications include: **ARGENTINA's** Computerworld Argentina, InfoWorld Argentina; **ASIA's** Computerworld Hong Kong, PC World Hong Kong, Computerworld Southeast Asia, PC World Singapore, Computerworld Malaysia, PC World Malaysia; **AUSTRALIA's** Computerworld Australia, Australian PC World, Australian Macworld, Network World, Reseller, IDG Sources; **AUSTRIA's** Computerwelt Oesterreich, PC Test; **BRAZIL's** Computerworld, Mundo IBM, Mundo Unix, PC World, Publish; **BULGARIA's** Computerworld Bulgaria, Ediworld, PC & Mac World Bulgaria; **CANADA's** Direct Access, Graduate Computerworld, InfoCanada, Network World Canada; **CHILE's** Computerworld, Informatica; **COLOMBIA's** Computerworld Colombia; **CZECH REPUBLIC's** Computerworld, Elektronika, PC World; **DENMARK's** CAD/CAM WORLD, Communications World, Computerworld Danmark, LOTUS World, Macintosh Produktkatalog, Macworld Danmark, PC World Danmark, PC World Produktguide, Windows World; **EQUADOR's** PC World; **EGYPT's** Computerworld (CW) Middle East, PC World Middle East; **FINLAND's** MikroPC, Tietoviikko, Tietoverkko; **FRANCE's** Distributique, GOLDEN MAC, InfoPC, Languages & Systems, Le Guide du Monde Informatique, Le Monde Informatique, Telecoms & Reseaux; **GERMANY's** Computerwoche, Computerwoche Focus, Computerwoche Extra, Computerwoche Karriere, Information Management, Macwelt, Netzwelt, PC Welt, PC Woche, Publish, Unit; **HUNGARY's** Alaplap, Computerworld SZT, PC World, ; **INDIA's** Computers & Communications; **ISRAEL's** Computerworld Israel, PC World Israel; **ITALY's** Computerworld Italia, Lotus Magazine, Macworld Italia, Networking Italia, PC World Italia; **JAPAN's** Computerworld Japan, Macworld Japan, SunWorld Japan, Windows World; **KENYA's** East African Computer News; **KOREA's** Computerworld Korea, Macworld Korea, PC World Korea; **MEXICO's** Compu Edicion, Compu Manufactura, Computacion/Punto de Venta, Computerworld Mexico, MacWorld, Mundo Unix, PC World, Windows; **THE NETHERLAND'S** Computer! Totaal, LAN Magazine, MacWorld; **NEW ZEALAND's** Computer Listings, Computerworld New Zealand, New Zealand PC World; **NIGERIA's** PC World Africa; **NORWAY's** Computerworld Norge, C/World, Lotusworld Norge, Macworld Norge, Networld, PC World Ekspress, PC World Norge, PC World's Product Guide, Publish World, Student Data, Unix World, Windowsworld, IDG Direct Response; **PANAMA's** PC World; **PERU's** Computerworld Peru, PC World; **PEOPLES REPUBLIC OF CHINA's** China Computerworld, PC World China, Electronics International, China Network World; **IDG HIGH TECH BEIJING's** New Product World; **IDG SHENZHEN's** Computer News Digest; **PHILLIPPINES'** Computerworld, PC World; **POLAND's** Computerworld Poland, PC World/ Komputer; **PORTUGAL's** Cerebro/PC World, Correio Informatico/Computerworld, MacIn; **ROMANIA's** PC World; **RUSSIA's** Computerworld-Moscow, Mir-PC, Sety; **SLOVENIA's** Monitor Magazine; **SOUTH AFRICA's** Computing S.A.; **SPAIN's** Amiga World, Computerworld Espana, Communicaciones World, Macworld Espana, PC World Espana, Publish, Sunworld; **SWEDEN's** Attack, ComputerSweden, Corporate Computing, Lokala Natverk/LAN, Lotus World, MAC&PC, Macworld, Mikrodatorn, PC World, Publishing & Design (CAP), Datalngenjoren, Maxi Data, Windows World; **SWITZERLAND's** Computerworld Schweiz, Macworld Schweiz, PC & Workstation; **TAIWAN's** Computerworld Taiwan, Global Computer Express, PC World Taiwan; **THAILAND's** Thai Computerworld; **TURKEY's** Computerworld Monitor, Macworld Turkiye, PC World Turkiye; **UNITED KINGDOM's** Lotus Magazine, Macworld, Sunworld; **UNITED STATES'** AmigaWorld, Cable in the Classroom, CD Review, CIO, Computerworld, Desktop Video World, DOS Resource Guide, Electronic News, Federal Computer Week, Federal Integrator, GamePro, IDGBooks, InfoWorld, InfoWorld Direct, Laser Event, Macworld, Multimedia World, Network World, NeXTWORLD, PC Games, PC Letter, PC World Publish, Sumeria, SunWorld, SWATPro, Video Event; **VENEZUELA's** Computerworld Venezuela, MicroComputerworld Venezuela; **VIETNAM's** PC World Vietnam.

Credits

Publisher
David Solomon

Managing Editor
Mary Bednarek

Acquisitions Editor
Janna Custer

Production Director
Beth Jenkins

Senior Editors
Tracy L. Barr
Sandy Blackthorn
Diane Graves Steele

Production Coordinator
Cindy L. Phipps

Acquisitions Assistant
Megg Bonar

Editorial Assistant
Darlene Cunningham

Editors
A. Timothy Gallan
Laurie Ann Smith

Technical Reviewer
Michael J. Partington

Production Staff
Tony Augsburger
Valery Bourke
Mary Breidenbach
Chris Collins
Sherry Gomoll
Drew Moore
Kathie Schnorr
Gina Scott

Proofreader
Kathleen Prata

Indexer
Sharon Hilgenberg

Contents at a Glance

Introduction

Well, now that the introductions are over, let's get down to it. The *Access 2 For Dummies Quick Reference* is a book that you can be proud to invite into your home or office. You can depend upon it to be there to explain each Access command that you'll use in your database. Want to learn more about a particular command? Look it up in the main part of the book, the Command Reference. For example, the Add Table command, which appears in the Relationships menu, is in the Rs section (Relationships⇨Add Table). The second part of this book, "A Toolbar Tour," shows you the mouse button shortcuts to your favorite commands. If you don't even know what a database is, then you'll find the last part of this book, the glossary, contains some of the basic terms that you need to know.

Access is a bit different from most of the programs you're used to working with. For one thing, unlike a word processor where you can open several documents at once, with Access you can only have one database open at a time. Within each database, however, you can open a number of different objects, each of which works with the same database information. For more information about this concept, look up the entry for the Database window, which also happens to be the first entry of the Command Reference.

Another thing that you may find surprising about Access is that the buttons that are available on the toolbar change depending upon what you're doing. If you're designing a form, you get a toolbar that's totally different from the one that you get when working with the actual information in the form. Again, for a summary of Access's toolbars and buttons, see the section "A Toolbar Tour."

One of the things that an Access Quick Reference needs to include is tips for making Access easier to use. (Otherwise, there wouldn't be anything quick about it.) You'll find that each command in this book lists any available shortcuts. Some commands have keyboard shortcuts; others have toolbar buttons; some have both.

Whether you're using this book to learn new tricks or just to refresh your memory, I hope you'll keep it by your computer for quick reference. If you're still trying to learn Access, you may want to pick up Scott Palmer's *Access 2 For Dummies*. It's got different jokes and walks you through the process of learning how to use Access. For the die-hard Access nerds, check out Prague and Irwin's *PC World Access 2 Bible, 2nd Edition*. It's chock-full of the advanced stuff that I haven't covered in this book (such as the Macro and Module features) and even some nit-picky basic info for beginners who want to know everything about Access.

That's really all you need to know about using this book. I hope it makes your experiences with Access just a little more pleasant.

What Do Those Pesky Icons Mean?

Oh, one more thing. This book is filled with funny little pictures designed to make comprehension a little easier. These pictures are called icons. The following list tells you what they signify:

 This icon flags commands that are recommended for the average Access user.

 This icon points out commands that are not recommended for the average Access user.

 This icon designates the kind of command that an average Access user may not want to use, but learning this command may come in handy.

 This icon flags commands that you can safely use.

 This icon flags commands that are usually safe, but if you're not careful, you may run into trouble.

 This icon designates commands that pose some danger to your data if you don't use them correctly, so be careful. You may be better off having someone else use these commands for you.

 This icon points out commands that you should never use unless you're some kind of programmer or technical guru.

 This icon warns of problem areas and potentially dangerous situations.

 This icon flags helpful information that will make life with Access easier.

 This icon points out little bits of information and trivia that may save your skin if you keep them in mind.

 This icon indicates a cross reference to another entry or section within this Quick Reference.

 This icon flags cross references to material in IDG's *Access 2 For Dummies.*

Part I

Command Reference

Database Window

Serves as the organizer for your database. Just like those little organizer notebooks, it has tabs on the side to let you pick what to work with. In this case, the tabs are for the various objects that make up a database — the tables, forms, reports, queries, and other stuff. You can use the Database window to open an existing object or create a new one.

You use the <u>W</u>indow⇨Database: *Name* command to move to the Database window. Substitute the name of your database for *Name*. (That kinda makes sense. Doesn't it?)

For mouse maniacs

 The Database window button is (almost) universally available and will take you to the Database window for the active database.

 On the Database window, click the Form button to take the first step in creating a new form or to look at existing forms. Click the New button at the top of the Database window to start creating a new form. (See <u>F</u>ile⇨Ne<u>w</u>.)

 On the Database window, click the Query button to take the first step in creating a new query or to look at existing queries. Click the New button at the top of the Database window to start creating a new query. (See <u>F</u>ile⇨Ne<u>w</u>.)

 On the Database window, click the Report button as the first step in creating a new report or to look at existing reports. Click the New button at the top of the Database window to start creating a new report. (See <u>F</u>ile⇨Ne<u>w</u>.)

 On the Database window, click the Table button as the first step in creating a new table or to list the tables of the current database. Click the New button at the top of the Database window to start creating a new table. (See <u>F</u>ile⇨Ne<u>w</u>.)

For keyboard krazies

This shortcut moves you to the Database window for the current database. If you don't have an F11 key, you can use Alt+F1.

Just the facts

The first step in using the Database window is to select the type of object that you want to work with using the tabs along the left side. Each tab represents one type of object — table, query, report, form, macro, or module. Simply click on the appropriate tab (or select the type of object from the View menu), and the corresponding list of objects is displayed. The following figure shows the forms associated with a database.

You'll use the objects differently: some you'll use only when designing your database; others you'll create as you need them; and you may invest the time to develop a library of yet others. As you work with your database, you'll probably develop a collection of reports and forms that you use repeatedly, and you'll use the Database window to select between them.

You use the buttons across the top of the Database window to work with the objects on the list. One of the most basic action is opening an existing table or form to work with the data it contains. You simply select the specific form (or table) that you want to work with and then click on the Open button. You can also just double-click on the object name.

Open The Open button lets you work with tables or forms for putting in data. Be sure that you select what you want to work with before you click on the button.

In the list of forms shown in the previous figure, you could work with the Address Book form either by selecting it and then clicking on the Open button or by double-clicking on the form's name.

New

One of two options that are available for all types of objects is the ability to create a new one. The first step is to pick what type of object you want (using the tabs on the left), and then you simply click on the New button. This step automatically takes you to the design screen for that type of object. (You'd better make sure that you have the right category of object (table, form, report, or whatever) selected before you click on the New button.)

Design

The other option that's always available is the capability to change the design of an existing object. Again, it's quite simple — simply select the object and click on the Design button. You need to have selected the object (table, form, report, or whatever) that you want to change before you click on this button, and you need to have highlighted the specific object, not just the category. You end up with the first one in the list by default.

If you want to base a new object on an existing one, simply open the old object and use File➪Save As to create a copy.

Preview

Reports are a special kind of object. Because of their complexity, you can't simply open a report for viewing. Instead, you use the Preview button to see what it will look like when printed. You can see what your report will look like by first selecting the report and then clicking on the Preview button.

Reports can be used to organize, group, and summarize your data and present it differently than the way it is stored. For simple calculations, such as finding the average of a field, you can use a query and the View➪Totals command, but in complex cases you'll want to use a report.

Run

The Run button appears only when working with macros or modules. You use this command to carry out the actions stored in the module or macro. These things are way too complex for an explanation on these little sheets of paper, so you'll just have to trust me that they work.

You may want to look at the *PC World Microsoft Access 2 Bible, 2nd Edition* for information on macros.

More stuff

When you are first creating your library of objects, it's important to use descriptive names. If you didn't, you can use the File➪Rename command to change the name of an existing object.

Once you've started working with a particular object, you use the View menu to move between working with the object and the corresponding design screen.

Look at the File⇨New entry to find some shortcuts for creating new forms, reports, queries, and tables. The Window⇨*List of open objects* command is used to move between parts of a database that have already been opened.

For an explanation of the objects that make up a database, see Chapter 2 of *Access 2 For Dummies*.

Edit⇨Clear Grid

Lets you start over with a new query. The *grid* holds all of the information defining your query.

Just the facts

Edit⇨Clear Grid isn't a command that you want to do by accident, so maybe that's why there isn't a shortcut for it. Basically, all you do is select the command, and all of the entries that you made on the query screen just disappear. (Don't worry too much if this happens. That's what Edit⇨Undo is there for.)

More stuff

If you just want to get rid of a piece of information within the grid, highlight it and then press the Delete key. If you want to clear out one field's information (one column), you can use Edit⇨Delete Column.

For more information about working with queries in general, try browsing through the commands that start with Query⇨, as they're the ones that control what your query actually does.

For more on setting up queries, see Chapter 12 of *Access 2 For Dummies*.

Edit⇨Clear Layout

Clears out the display of the relationships that exist between tables within your database. In reality, clearing the layout isn't a problem as long as you don't save the changes (which would get rid of the relationships). However, if someone else built the database for you, you should probably avoid this command just to be on the safe side (usually upwind). After all, you don't want to destroy their relationships. That's the sort of thing that really upsets database gurus. If it's your own database, feel free to wipe everything out and start over. You use this command when you are changing the graphical display of the relationships (links) between the tables in your database.

Just the facts

This command is really a shortcut for starting over when you are creating the relationships in a database. You will most often use Edit⇨Clear Layout when you've been changing the relationships and realize that the way they're organized on-screen makes it harder to track what's going on. Rather than move each table individually, you may decide to clear them all out and add them back in one by one in an order that makes sense.

See Relationships⇨Edit Relationship for a sample of the display.

More stuff

If you clear out all of the relationships, there is no easy way to recreate them. That's why it's a good idea to have a printout of the relationships within your database. To get one, use File⇨Print Definition. Fortunately, the changes aren't saved unless you select File⇨Save Layout.

To get rid of a single relationship, select the line representing the relationship and press the Delete key.

To add the tables back in, you'll need to use Relationships⇨Add Table. If a relationship already exists between two tables, the line representing it will appear when you add the second table.

Edit⇨Copy

Makes a copy of whatever you have selected and puts it onto the Clipboard (a super-secret nerd place). You use this command (with Edit⇨Paste) for making more than one copy of existing information.

For mouse maniacs

The Copy button is a perennial favorite; just be sure that you have something highlighted first. The button isn't available everywhere, but it is there whenever you are likely to be editing the actual database contents.

For keyboard krazies

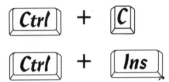

Just the facts

There are basically four steps (and two commands) involved in using Edit⇨Copy. The first step is to highlight the information that you want to make a copy of. Next, select Edit⇨Copy. This action puts a copy of whatever you had highlighted onto the Clipboard. You then need to move to where you want the new copy of the information. You can use any of the methods that you know for moving, none of which will change what's on the Clipboard. To actually insert the information from the Clipboard, select Edit⇨Paste. That's all there is to it. If you want to put the information in more than one spot, simply move to another location and select Edit⇨Paste again. You can paste as many times as you want to make your copies. Note that only one thing can be on the Clipboard at a time. If you copy (or cut) something new, the old information is thrown out.

More stuff

You can use the Copy command to copy the information from several fields into a new record, or you can copy an entire record. If you want to make a new record, you need to use Edit⇨Paste Append rather than the plain old Edit⇨Paste.

The Cut, Copy, and Paste commands can also be used to move information between programs. With these commands, you get a copy of the data inserted into your database. The copy is formatted by Access and is totally independent of the original program. In fact, you can throw the original away or change it completely. In contrast, with the Edit⇨Insert Object command, Access and the other program remain in touch using OLE, which means that any changes in the original are automatically included in your database.

You can use the Copy and Paste command to duplicate objects at the Database window or to copy objects from one database to another. You can use Cut and Paste to move an object to another database. When you paste the object, you may be prompted with a Paste As dialog box. For example, when pasting tables, you have a choice between copying the table complete with data or creating a new blank table with the same structure.

You may want to check out Copy's partners, Edit⇨Cut and Edit⇨Paste.

See Chapter 8 of *Access 2 For Dummies* for information on having Access automatically insert a value when you are creating a new record (rather than copying the information from somewhere else).

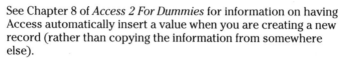

Edit⇨Cut

Takes whatever you have selected and puts it onto the Clipboard (a super-secret nerd place). You use this command (along with Edit⇨Paste) to move information.

For mouse maniacs

Dig those little scissors. Even though the Cut command is available throughout Access, the Cut button is only on toolbars where you are editing data.

For keyboard krazies

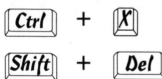

Just the facts

There are basically four steps (and two commands) involved in using Edit⇨Cut. The first step is to let Access know what information you want to work with by highlighting what you want to move. Next, select Edit⇨Cut. What you had highlighted disappears and is stored on the Clipboard. You then need to move to where you want to put the information. You can use any of the methods that you know for moving, as none of them will change what's on the Clipboard. To actually insert the information, select Edit⇨Paste. That's all there is to it. The information is gone from its old position and inserted where you now want it. Remember that only one thing can be on the Clipboard at a time. If you copy (or cut) something new, the old information on the Clipboard is thrown out.

Just like with Edit⇨Copy, you can put the information in more than one spot. Simply move to another location and select Edit⇨Paste again. You can paste as many times as you want to make your new copies. Also, if you want to replace some old information with what you have just copied, highlight the old information before selecting Edit⇨Paste.

More stuff

You can use the Cut command to move information from one record to another. If you want to make a new record with the information, you need to use Edit⇨Paste Append rather the plain old Edit⇨Paste. You may use this method if, for example, two of your friends get divorced and you need to make a new record for each of them in your address book (rather than having them on a single record).

If you want to make a copy of what you have selected, you'd use Edit⇨Copy. You use Edit⇨Paste to put whatever's on the Clipboard into your document. Although Cut and Paste can also be used to move information between programs, it's generally better to use Edit⇨Copy.

Edit⇨Delete

Gets rid of whatever is selected. This command can be problematic if you confuse it with Edit⇨Cut.

For keyboard krazies

Just the facts

This command is (unfortunately) one of the easiest commands to use. Just highlight what you want to get rid of and press the Delete key. It's a real bummer to have something highlighted, reach for another key, and hit Delete by mistake. If that happens to you, use Edit⇨Undo right away.

More stuff

If you want to move highlighted information somewhere else, you should probably use Edit⇨Cut.

Edit⇨Delete Column

Removes a field (and the associated information) when designing a new query or redesigning an existing query. There are always blank columns at the right of a query, so you can add the field back in if you want.

Just the facts

You'll first need to highlight a portion of a column that you want to get rid of. It's enough to be in just one row of the column. To highlight a group of side-by-side columns, either drag your mouse across a row or hold down the Shift key and use your arrow keys to add new columns to your selection. After you have the columns selected, just go up to the menu and pick Edit⇨Delete Column to get rid of them.

More stuff

Be careful when you're using this command, as it's very easy to get rid of something that you may need later, and it's very difficult to bring it back. (Unless you notice your mistake right away and use Edit⇨Undo.)

If you want to start over and get rid of everything in a query, use Edit⇨Clear Grid.

For more on setting up queries, see Chapter 12 of Access 2 For Dummies.

Edit⇨Delete Row

Gets rid of a field definition when you're designing a table or a criteria when you are working with queries.

For mouse maniacs

The Delete Row button is only available when you are designing a table.

Just the facts

This is a pretty straight-forward command. Whatever row that you are in when you select Edit⇨Delete Row goes away. In a query, the rule represented by a deleted row is no longer used when selecting records. In a table definition, that field is gone.

More stuff

The problem with this command is that if you are working with a table definition and get rid of a row, it means that you've just gotten rid of a field and all of the information in it. Be sure that you really mean to throw all of that stuff out before you select this command. Otherwise, you may find yourself typing everyone's phone number in again (or whatever field you happened to delete).

Well, I suppose that I should mention this command's companion, Edit➪Insert Row. You may also want to look at Edit➪Delete Column because it's much more useful (most of the time).

Edit➪Duplicate

Makes another copy of some part of a form or report right next to the first one. It's a little bit faster than using Edit➪Copy and then Edit➪Paste when you need several copies of some object that you've modified (added a fancy border and made it purple, say). You'll find that this command is available when you are designing the layout for a report or form.

Just the facts

This command is actually itself a shortcut for Copy and Paste, so you don't get a shortcut for a shortcut. To use it, simply select the control (or controls) that you want to duplicate and then go to the menu and pick the command. You'll get a new copy of the selected controls slightly offset from the original. Now you have to move the controls to their new location.

More stuff

Rather than move each control by hand, you can use Format➪Align, Format➪Vertical Spacing, and Format➪Horizontal Spacing to distribute them evenly. This method is particularly useful when you are trying to create a group of controls. Use Edit➪Duplicate to make as many controls as you need, Format➪Vertical Spacing to stack them evenly, and then Format➪Align to make them line up neatly.

If you use Edit➪Copy and Edit➪Paste, you'll have more control over where the next copies are placed.

See Chapter 14 of *Access 2 For Dummies* for information about customizing your forms to look the way you want.

Edit⇨Find

Works as a quick search for finding a record with matching information. This command is much faster, but less powerful, than writing a query. In fact, one of its uses is for finding a specific record when you're looking at your query results and discover that you ended up with more records than you expected.

For mouse maniacs

  Well, click the Find button and find anything.

For keyboard krazies

F7 opens the Find dialog box, but an even more useful shortcut is Shift+F4, which repeats the previous Find or Replace action.

Just the facts

Although the standard way of searching for information in your database is to use a query, there are two methods that are often faster and more suited for quick searches. One is the creation of a filter that limits which records are displayed. (For more information, see Records⇨Edit Filter/Sort). The other is through the use of the Find command.

Find is actually very easy to use. If you know which field contains the information that you are looking for (for example, someone's last name is probably in the Last Name field), you should first go to that field. Don't worry about which record you are currently on, just which field you're in.

The next step is to select Edit⇨Find which reveals the wonderful, wacky Find dialog box. In general, the name of the dialog box will include the name of the current field when you first open it.

After the dialog box is open, you need to tell Access what it is you're looking for. You do that by typing information in the Find What text box. When the dialog box first opens, that's where you are, so you can just start typing. Any old information will be highlighted and will disappear with your first letter.

If you want to find a record that contains that text as the entire contents of the current field without paying attention to capitals or formatting, yon can just click on the Find First button. If you want to have more control, there's a bit more to learn.

To exercise your new found control, you must make some decisions about how Find should go about doing its job. First, do you want it to search just the current field or every field in the database? You need to pick one by clicking on either of the two choices in the Search in area, which is why you needed to move to the correct field first — Access only lets you pick the current field or all of them. You can't change your mind once you open the box. Of course, you can close the box, move to the right field, and then select Edit⇨Find again. The text you typed will still be in the Find What text box.

You need to tell Access whether to search for the text that you typed only at the start of a field, anywhere within the field, or if the text must be the entire field. An example may help here (I hope so because I bothered writing one):

Imagine that you are looking for a friend whom you call "Beth." Now, if you know that that's her real name and that that's how it's entered into the database, you could select Match Whole Field and be sure to find her. (The field must contain "Beth" and only "Beth.") But what if you know her name is either "Beth" or "Bethany," and you're not sure which. Well, both possibilities start with "Beth" so you need to use the Start Of Field option to find either. Of course, this search wouldn't find "Elizabeth." To be sure to find all three possibilities (Beth, Bethany or Elizabeth), you need to search for "Beth" using the Any Part Of Field option.

The preceding example raises another issue. You can also tell Access to make sure that the text matches the way you have it capitalized. This feature is useful if you are certain that the name you are looking for is written in all caps (IDG BOOKS rather than IDG Books or IDG books). In the example, if you selected the Match Case option, "Beth" would never match "Elizabeth," and "beth" would never match either "Beth" or "Bethany." The case (B versus b) would have to be the same for Access to consider it a match.

The final option that controls what Access looks for is Search Fields as Formatted. This option can be a bit complex to figure out, but basically the way information is displayed in a field may be different from what you actually typed in or what is stored by Access. For example, dates can be displayed a great many ways, but they are not stored with the day of the week. (Don't worry about how they are stored; just trust me that the day of the week is not part of the information.) If you want to search for a date that you know was on a Saturday (because your evil boss made you work over the weekend), you need to type "Saturday" as the Find What text and select Search Fields as Formatted. Access will find the Saturday dates even though it has to figure out that day of the week from the stored date. A word of warning: this procedure only works with the way data is currently being displayed. For this example to work, you need to have formatted the date field to include the day of the week in the display.

If you have an idea of where the record is located, you can speed up your search by telling Access to search up towards the first record or down towards the last record. Select either Up or Down in the Direction area to go ahead and point Access in the right direction. (These directions are based on how the records are displayed in the datasheet.) If Access gets to the beginning (or end) without finding a match, it will go ahead and search the remaining records.

More stuff

Although you can use Find with a datasheet or a form, each method has its advantages. A datasheet (the normal view for a table or the results of a query) let you see those records around the one you found, which is useful if you need to compare the records. The information presented in a form is a bit easier to read (assuming that the form is well designed).

If you're not exactly sure what you are looking for, you can use *wildcards*. For those of you who don't play poker, a wildcard can stand in for any other card (or, in this case, character). There are several different wildcard characters that can be used with Find. The simplest is the question mark (?) which can represent any one character. The standard example (which I'll use because I'm too tired to be creative) is using "Sm?th" to match either "Smith" or "Smyth." In a similar fashion, you can use the pound sign (#) to represent any single digit. For example, if you know someone is in his thirties, you could search for 3# and find any number between 30 and 39. The asterisk (*) wildcard matches any number of characters. For example, "d*g" matches either "dog" or "dawg." Unlike DOS or Windows, in Access you can anchor both ends of a word with the asterisk in the middle.

A slightly more advanced technique is to use the square brackets ([]) to surround a group of choices. The text "[bf]at" matches either "bat" or "fat." You can also specify ranges within brackets by using the hyphen (-) so that "[b-f]at" matches "bat," "cat," "eat," and "fat." (It would match "dat" as well, but that isn't a word!) Finally, you can use the exclamation point (!) within the brackets to mean not. The text "[!b]at" would match every possible three letter word ending in "at" except for "bat."

Spelling counts! Be careful both when you are typing in the original data and when filling in what it is you want to search for. You'd never find your pet "Dog" by searching for "Dawg." On the plus side, you only need part of the information: "Dog" does turn up if you just ask for "Do."

Setting a field as Indexed speeds up searches involving that field. To set a field as Indexed, you need to go to the table design and select the field. Down at the bottom is an option for Indexed, which you can set to either Yes (Duplicates OK) or Yes (No Duplicates).

If you want to find matches for a word or phrase and replace the matches with something else, use Edit⇨Replace.

For a quick introduction to the query screen, see Chapter 11 and Chapter 12 of *Access 2 For Dummies*.

Edit⇨Insert Column

Puts a new, blank column into a query design. This command is important because the order of the fields in the query determines the order of the fields.

Just the facts

Is it discrimination that the Insert Row command has a button and Insert Column doesn't? Anyway, the Insert Column command is still pretty easy to use. Go to the column to the right of where you want the new, blank column and then select the command. What could be simpler? OK, those new mind-reading computers that will be on the market right after you buy your next computer, but that's in the future.

More stuff

Be careful to avoid creating duplicate columns. Not only do duplicates make your query results look funny, but it's much more complex to figure out what your doing when you have the same field in more than one column. If you need to use more than one rule for a particular field, then add a row to the criteria section.

Let's see, there's the Edit⇨Insert Row command for adding a field or criteria and then the Edit⇨Delete Column and Edit⇨Delete Row commands for getting rid of them.

Edit⇨Insert Object

Puts an object (which is just about anything) into your database. This feature is part of OLE (Object Linking and Embedding) and is pretty nerdy stuff. Basically, it lets you add in something created in another program. If you link to the object, the object exists as a file on disk. If you embed the object, it is included as part of your database. Although not as dangerous as bullfighting, OLE is part of the very newest Windows technology (and therefore more likely to break).

Just the facts

The first thing to understand is that there is a big difference between inserting an object onto a form or report when you are designing it and inserting an object into a field. In the first case (adding an object to your design), you're just inserting that object as part of the background of the report or form. A simple example would be a logo that appears at the top of a report. If the logo is changed (by those zany folks over in the art department), your copy can be automatically updated. A more sophisticated example might be an icon on the top of the form that, when you click it, tells you with a recorded sound about the form. Because the sound requires another program to play it, it needs to be an OLE object. Microsoft refers to this type of object as *unbounded*.

If you create a field of the OLE object type, you can create what Microsoft calls a *bounded* object. Basically, a bounded object can be different for each record. A common example (though in reality somewhat unrealistic) is that every record in the personnel file contains a sample of the individual's voice. Each voice is different, so the object is in a field rather than on the background. There are tremendous advantages to using OLE for sophisticated databases, but they are more than what normal folk ever need worry about.

However, since you paid your money, I'll give you a quick overview of inserting objects. Fortunately, after you've figured out whether you're working with an object as part of the design of a report or form or an object as something in your database, you follow the same basic steps. First, go to where you want the object and select Edit⇨Insert Object. You get the following dialog box:

Talk about your involved dialog boxes. The contents of this one changes based on what you have installed on your computer, but the process is fairly straightforward once you decide what type of object you want.

To use an object that already exists as a file on your system, click on the Create From File button. You can then use the dialog box to find the file containing the object. After you've found it, double-click on it (or highlight it and press Enter) to actually insert it as an object. Access will be able to figure what type of object you just inserted.

To create a new object that will just exist within your database, you need to start by selecting the Create New option and telling Access what type of object you want in the Object Type list. Highlight the object type (based on the program that will create it, such as an Excel Spreadsheet) and click on OK (or press Enter). You're now in the other program that will create the object. Do whatever you need to create the object (after buying the appropriate *For Dummies* book and its accompanying *Dummies Quick Reference*) and then select the last command on the File menu. It's probably something like Exit and Return to Access Database. That's it. The object has been inserted.

More stuff

There's another decision that you have to make along the way: whether to display the actual object or an icon representing the object. The Display As Icon option can be very useful when you are using an OLE object as the contents of a field. For example, imagine that each record in a museum database contains a picture of the item it discusses. The pictures may be of various sizes and shapes. Rather than trying to design a form that can display the pictures no matter what size they are, you may decide to use an icon instead. The icon is the same size on each record, which simplifies your form design. To see the picture, you just double-click on the icon. By using icons, your system works faster because it doesn't have to draw a complex picture each time you switch records. Some objects (such as sounds) have to be displayed as icons.

The Object Type list can include programs that you once had but are now deleted (or at least temporarily taken off of your system). The problem is that the available objects are registered when a program is added and there isn't a standard way to remove them. Just restrict your choices to the programs on your machine.

Using Edit⇨Paste Special is another OLE method.

Edit➪Insert Row

Adds a row to the criteria region of a query or inserts a blank row for a field definition when designing a table. The whole point is that you can insert the new stuff where you want rather than at the end. Move to the spot where you want to insert the row before selecting the command.

For mouse maniacs

The Insert Row button is available only when you are designing a table.

Just the facts

Go to the row that you want to move down and select Edit➪Insert Row (or click the Insert Row button). The row that you are in will move down and a new, blank row will appear above it.

More stuff

You really don't have to worry about the order that you enter field definitions in a table. Each datasheet where you view the data can have its own arrangement that is independent of the order of the definitions. You can also move field definitions after they've been entered by dragging them to a new location.

Edit➪Delete Row lets you get rid of a field definition or a line in the criteria region. If you're trying to add the Totals row to your query design, you need to use View➪Totals.

The situations where you will use multiple rows in a query are discussed in Chapter 13 of *Access 2 For Dummies.*

Edit➪Links

Changes where Access looks for the files containing linked objects and lets you manage how Access updates information via those links. You only have linked objects if you are using OLE to include information that is actually stored in a file created by another program.

Just the facts

Changing where Access looks for the files used by an OLE link is very easy. All you have to do is select the Edit➪Links command and you're shown a dialog box listing all of the existing links.

You can then select which link to work with by clicking on it. To change which file Access is using for the information, select Change Source button in the Edit Links dialog box. You can then move around on your hard disk until you find the new file that you want to use.

You can also use the Edit Link dialog box to break a link by using the Break Link button. When you break an OLE link, the information is permanently inserted into your document and cannot be edited by the original program.

In some cases, you may have to create a link that requires you to manually update the information. This situation is true of all bound objects (information that is inserted into a field of the OLE object type). Simply select the link and click on the Update Now button. The information that is currently in the linked file will be used to update the field.

More stuff

When a field is displaying information contained in a linked file, accidentally deleting the file will not cause the image to change. You will, however, run into problems if you try to update that link manually. Because the file no longer exists, Access won't be able to find any information, and the object will be deleted. With objects that are in the background (unbounded), you have more of problem because Access will try to update the link automatically when you first open the form or report. If you intend to delete the link to a file, you should break the link first so that a copy of the information remains in Access.

If you have a group of files that are used as objects in your database, you may want to create a special subdirectory for them. That way, if you need to move the database to another system, you can copy all of the linked files easily. When first creating the link, move the file to the subdirectory first. Otherwise, you'll have to use Edit⇨Links to change the link after you move the file.

If you want to edit a linked object, simply double-click on the object (or select the object and use Edit⇨Object). The program that created the object will open (assuming that it is available).

Before you use Edit⇨Links, you must have already created a link using either Edit⇨Insert Object or Edit⇨Paste Special.

Edit⇨Object

Opens the proper program to edit an OLE object (something created in a different program). It doesn't matter if the object is linked or embedded, this command will still work. (In most cases, so will double-clicking on the object.)

Just the facts

You just need to select the object that you want to edit and select Edit⇨Object. Be warned that the name of the command changes to reflect the type of object that you're going to be working with (Excel Spreadsheet Object or Paintbrush Picture Object).

More stuff

For most images, double-clicking will open the program that created the object and allow you to make changes. For objects that have actions (such as playing sound or showing animation), double-clicking will start the action. You'll need to use the menu in order to edit the object.

See Edit⇨Links for information about changing where Access looks for the linked file and Edit⇨Insert Object or Edit⇨Paste Special for information about adding an OLE object.

Edit⇨Paste

Inserts whatever is currently on the Clipboard. You put things onto the Clipboard by using either the Edit⇨Cut or Edit⇨Paste command. You can keep selecting Edit⇨Paste to insert multiple copies.

For mouse maniacs

One click of the Paste button inserts whatever you cut or copied last. The button is only available when working with datasheets.

For keyboard krazies

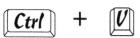

Just the facts

In order for this command to do any good, you must have put something onto the Clipboard by using either Edit⇨Copy or Edit⇨Cut. The Edit⇨Paste command takes the contents of the Clipboard and inserts it at the cursor. The only restriction is that if you are pasting it into a field, Access must be able to convert the information to the proper format for the field type. You can paste the same thing into different locations as many times as you want.

More stuff

The information that you are pasting can be part of the contents of a field, one or more entire fields, an entire record, a control, or even information from another program. The only requirement is that the location is of the right type to hold the pasted information. In other words, you can't paste a picture into a field designed to hold text.

If you have anything selected, Edit⇨Paste will replace that information with whatever is in the Clipboard.

If you're working with a datasheet (the standard view of a table or the results of a query), the information is pasted based upon shape. If there is information that won't fit (for example, you're on the last row and the Clipboard contains two rows worth of information), the "extra" information will just be dropped. It's still on the Clipboard, but it won't be added to your document. If you are working with a form and have information on the Clipboard that was contained in fields that don't exist on the form, the information for those fields will be dropped (though they're still on the Clipboard).

Use Edit⇨Cut and Edit⇨Copy to put things onto the Clipboard. Edit⇨Paste Special creates an OLE object out of whatever is on the Clipboard, and Edit⇨Paste Append is used when you are copying or moving an entire record and want to create a new record rather than replace the existing information.

Edit⇨Paste Append

Inserts whatever is on the clipboard as a new record instead of replacing the information in the current record.

Just the facts

You use this command exactly like the Edit⇨Paste command. As with Edit⇨Paste, you have to have first put something onto the Clipboard by using either Edit⇨Cut or Edit⇨Copy. The only difference is that Paste Append uses the information to create new records at the end of the datasheet.

"Only" is a bit misleading here because the difference can be quite important. For example, if you are adding notes to a database, you may want the same information on several records. If you highlight the field containing the text and select Edit⇨Copy, the information is put onto the Clipboard. Now if you go to another record and select Edit⇨Paste, the information will be inserted into the proper field. On the other hand, if you select Edit⇨Paste Append, you'd end up with a new record containing just that information.

More stuff

There are two cases where Edit⇨Paste Append is of tremendous value. When you want to duplicate a record, simply select the entire record (use Edit⇨Select Record) and make a copy using Edit⇨Copy. Then select Edit⇨Paste Append. You end up with a new copy of the record at the end of your datasheet. When you are bringing information in from another program, use Edit⇨Copy in that program to put the information on the Clipboard and use Edit⇨Paste Append within Access to create a new record for each row of information.

If you want to replace what's already present with what's on the Clipboard, use Edit⇨Paste.

Edit⇨Paste Special

Creates an OLE object with the contents of the Clipboard. In general, you want what's on the Clipboard to have come from a different program. An OLE object is only sorta inserted into your database. You need to use the original program that created the object in order to make any changes.

Just the facts

The first step is to have put the information (whether its a picture, sounds, or whatever) onto the Clipboard. You do this by using Edit⇨Copy in the program where you created the stuff. (You can use Edit⇨Cut, but it's generally better to leave the original and use Copy instead.)

After you choose the location within your Access database for the new information, simply select Edit⇨Paste Special and then click on the Paste Link button. You then pick the type of object that you're working with from the list, but in almost all cases, Access will have guessed correctly and you can just click OK.

More stuff

You can also use Paste Special to convert the information on the Clipboard into a different format. In general, there is no point in making such a change, but sometimes a different format will provide better performance or make graphics appear crisper. To use a different format, simply click on the Paste button and select the new format from the list.

If the information that you want to paste is stored in a file, you can use Edit⇨Insert Object instead (and you don't have to bother with the Clipboard).

Edit⇨Relationships

Adds the Relationships menu and lets you change the links between your tables. Any time you're at a Database window, this command is there for you.

For mouse maniacs

One click of the Relationships button and you're off into the troubled world of database design.

Just the facts

The only purpose of this command is to open the visual display of the relationships within your database. Sometimes it's pretty cool to look at, but you want to be careful not to change anything unless you know what you're doing. For more information about the display, see Relationships⇨Edit Relationship.

More stuff

The commands on the Relationships menu are discussed over in the R's because they all start with Relationships⇨. The other command that you may want to look at is Edit⇨Clear Layout, which gets rid of the display of relationships shown on the layout.

Relationships (at least within databases) are discussed in Chapter 18 of *Access 2 For Dummies*.

Edit⇨Replace

Locates matches for a word or phrase and then lets you replace that word or phrase with something else. This feature is most useful when you misspelled the same word fifty times and now you need to fix it.

For mouse maniacs

The Replace button doesn't appear on any toolbar until you add it, but it's useful enough to mention.

For keyboard krazies

 +

Shift+F7 opens the Replace dialog box, but an even more useful shortcut is Shift+F4 which repeats the previous Find or Replace action.

Just the facts

Edit⇨Replace is basically the Edit⇨Find command with an attitude. Replace only works with the current field, so make sure that you moved to the right field before selecting the command. In addition to the Find What text box, there's a Replace With box. Fill in what you want the new information to be in the Replace With box and you're all set.

One word of caution: Replace always searches for a match anywhere within the field. If you change "dog" to "cat," you'll also change "doghouse" to "cathouse." Be very careful with the Replace All button. It's usually better to use Find Next and Replace to move from one match to another.

More stuff

See Edit⇨Find for more information about how the actual search works. You can have much greater control over the changes that you are making by using an Update query. (See Query⇨Update.)

Chapter 13 of *Access 2 For Dummies* contains an introduction to changing information by using an action query.

Edit⇨Select All

Selects all of the objects *within* the current layout. Whatever command that you do next will affect everything.

For keyboard krazies

Just the facts

This one's real easy. Just go to the menu and select the command. Generally, you'll use Edit⇨Select All with the commands on the Format menu, or you'll change a setting on the Palette (such as the background color). Because everything is selected, each control will be changed to the new setting, which is important if you want to give your forms or reports a consistent look.

More stuff

Edit⇨Select All only works to select the controls on the form or report. If you want to select the entire form (or the entire report) to change its properties, you must use Select Form (or Select Report). If you're looking at the data, you'll be able select the actual data by using either Edit⇨Select All Records or Edit⇨Select Record. For more information on using the tools on the Palette, see View⇨Palette.

Edit⇨Select All Records

Selects all of the records in the group being displayed. If you are using a query, only those records that are part of the result are selected. After selecting all records, you can then use a command and have it affect all of the records. (Delete is probably a bad choice.)

For keyboard krazies

Just the facts

Just select Edit⇨Select All Records, and all of the information in the current table is selected. You can now use any command that's available, and it will affect all of the data. If you're working with a form (or report), all of the records in all of the tables used by the form or report will be selected.

More stuff

Don't select Edit⇨Delete after selecting all records unless you just got fired and want to destroy everything. With everything selected, Edit⇨Delete would remove all of the information from the table. Usually that's a very bad thing.

To just select everything on the current record, use Edit⇨Select Record.

Edit⇨Select Form

Selects the form itself so that you can access the form properties. You can also get to the form properties by double-clicking in the gray region outside of the form. This command is only available when you are designing a form.

For mouse maniacs

To select the form with the mouse, click on the corner where the two rulers meet in the upper-left. For those of you not interested in target practice, you can also click anywhere in the gray area outside of the form.

Just the facts

The main reason that you want to use this command is to get the form's properties. To do this task, first select the form (using Edit⇨Select Form) and then view the properties (using View⇨Properties).

One of the most useful properties is DefaultView, which tells Access how to display multiple forms. If you select Single Form, each record is on its own screen. If you select Continuous Form, Access behaves as though the forms are printed on a single, long sheet of paper. The final option is Datasheet, which ignores the form and shows the information in the datasheet grid.

Another property you may want to set is DefaultEditing, which is most useful if someone else is gong to be using your form. You can use the Read Only option to really annoy anyone else who works with the data because no one will be able to change anything in the database (which is great if that's what you intend). If you set the property to Data Entry, you'll get a new, blank form every time you open the form. Allow Edits is the default setting; it lets you change things. You need to use Records⇨Data Entry to add records (or go to the last record in the database). The final option, Can't Add Records, is pretty obvious: you can change things but not add new records.

More stuff

 To work with the objects on the form, you need to use Edit⇨Select All. To work with the data within a form, you must move out of the design view and then you can use either Edit⇨Select Record or Edit⇨Select All Records.

 Edit⇨Select Record

Selects just the data contained within the current record. You can then use any command that affects the contents of fields.

For keyboard krazies

Shift + **Space**

Just the facts

When you select this command, the entire record is highlighted and ready for your next action. That's all there is to it. The hard part is figuring out what command you want to use next.

More stuff

 One of the reasons for using this command is to make a duplicate record. After you've selected the entire record, select Edit⇨Copy and Edit⇨Paste Append. You need to use Paste Append (rather than plain old Paste) in order to create a new record.

 If you want to select all of the records, use Edit⇨Select All Records.

Edit⇨Select Report

Selects the actual report design so that you can change its
properties. You can also access the report properties by clicking
in the gray region outside the report boundaries. This command
is only available when you are designing a report.

For mouse maniacs

To select the report design, click on the corner where the two
rulers meet in the upper-left. For those of you not interested in
target practice, you can also click anywhere in the gray area
outside of the form.

Just the facts

You use the Edit⇨Select Report command as the first step in
getting to a report's properties. The second step is to select
View⇨Properties.

More stuff

If you are working with a form, the command is Edit⇨Select Form.
To work with the objects on the report, you need to use
Edit⇨Select All. If you want to select the data within a report, use
either Edit⇨Select Record or Edit⇨Select All Records.

Edit⇨Set Primary Key

Determines which field is the primary key for the table. You can
only have one primary key per table. Basically, the primary key
must be different for each record; it determines the order used
when listing the records. This command is only available when
you are designing a table.

For mouse maniacs

When you use the Set Primary Key button, make sure that you're
in the field where you want to make the primary key.

Just the facts

You need to move to the row containing the field definition for
the field that you want to use as the primary key. When you select
Edit⇨Set Primary Key, the current field becomes the primary key

(you'll see the little key icon on the left). Because you can have only one primary key in a table, any other field that was set as the primary key is reset to a normal field.

More stuff

Because the primary key must be unique (different) for each record, it's often best to use a counter field as your primary key. The value for a counter field is provided by Access and automatically increases by one each time you create a new record. If the real-world source for the information in your database contains an identifying code, you can use that field as the primary key. For example, with people, the social security number is always unique and could be used as the primary key. In a system designed to track invoices, you could use the invoice number as the primary key as long as you are sure that you will never have two invoices with the same number.

Setting a field as the primary key results in faster searches of that field. You can get the same benefit by setting the Indexed property for the field (down in the bottom left of the table design screen) to either Yes (Duplicates OK) or Yes (No Duplicates). Primary keys are always set to Yes (No Duplicates).

If you often sort your database on a field other than the primary key, you may want to index that field. See View⇨Indexes for more information.

The importance of a primary key is touched upon in Chapter 4 of *Access 2 For Dummies*.

Edit⇨Tab Order

Determines the order that you visit fields when pressing the tab key. This command lets you control the order that you enter information in your form. The better the organization, the easier it is to enter data. This command is only available when you are designing a form.

Just the facts

It's generally easier to set the tab order as one of the last things you do when designing a form. (Maybe that's why there isn't any shortcut.) Once you select the command, the dialog box is displayed listing all of the fields in the form.

To change the tab order, simply click once on the left of the field name (in that little box) to select the field and then drag the field to its new position. You can also select a group of fields by clicking on the first one and dragging the selection through the group.

More stuff

The normal order for moving between fields is left-to-right, top-to-bottom. Simply select the Auto Order button to put the fields in that proper order. It's often easier to first organize the fields this way and then move those that you want in a different order.

If you want to skip over a field, you need to select the control and then View⇨Properties. Set the TabStop property to No.

Edit⇨Undo

Backs you up one step. Remember, this command is your friend. This is the command that I would nominate as being the most important in making computers friendlier. Any action that changes your data within the database can be undone. Some actions that involve files (such as saving) can't be undone.

For mouse maniacs

The Undo button is also known as the "Help! Get me out of here!" button.

For keyboard krazies

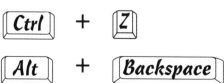

Just the facts

As long as you remember to do it immediately after a mistake, all you need to do is go to the Edit menu and select the Undo command. Or better yet, just use one of the shortcuts.

More stuff

The actual command name changes to indicate what the last action was (the one that can be undone). Typical command names are Undo Typing, Undo Cut, Undo Paste, and Undo Saved Record.

The Undo Current Field/Record command is a separate command that undoes changes that have been made to the current record. The Undo Saved Record command (which is just one version of the standard Undo) is only available immediately after you move away from a record in which the contents have been changed.

Edit⇨Undo Current Field/Record

Lets you undo any changes you made to the current record (as long as you select the command before moving to a new record). Very often there will be a series of changes to the same record. The standard Edit⇨Undo command will only reverse the most recent change. Unfortunately, this could be a problem if you suddenly realize that you've been making changes to the wrong record. That's why there's the Undo Current Record (or Undo Current Field) command.

For mouse maniacs

The Undo Record/Field button is a true lifesaver. OK. May be just a true data saver, but important nonetheless.

For keyboard krazies

Just the facts

The name of the button and command changes based on whether you are in a field that you just changed or whether you moved somewhere else within the same record. To undo the changes that you've made to the current record, simply select the command (or one of the shortcuts).

More stuff

 Changes to the contents of your database are automatically
stored as you move away from the record containing a change.
This feature minimizes the chance that you'll lose large amounts
of data. If you have just moved away from a changed record (and
haven't done anything else), you will be able to select Edit⇨Undo
Saved Record to get back the original record.

Expression Builder

Helps you build expressions. You use expressions for calculating
values to be automatically inserted into a field, updating data, and
developing rules for use in searching through data. Although
difficult to get used to, the Expression Builder actually does make
using your database easier. No command is available for Expression Builder on any of the drop-down menus, but when the
Expression Builder is available, the Build command shows up on
the right-button menu.

For mouse maniacs

 This Build button is a little bit tricky because what opens when
you click on it depends on where you are. If a small version of the
button appears at the end of the text box when you are working
with a query, clicking it will get you the Expression Builder. The
larger version of the button on the toolbar usually opens a
Wizard.

Just the facts

You can use the Expression Builder to create criteria for queries
or filters, calculate values for use in fields, or define validation
rules. You'll usually have the option opening the Expression
Builder whenever you are in a text box that can be filled with
either a single value or a logical rule. Often, the button for the
Expression Builder appears at the right of the text box rather
than on the toolbar. Once you click on the button, the Expression
Builder opens to reveal the following dialog box:

These four buttons
are used for math.

These four buttons are
the "logical operator"
symbols—equals, greater
than, less than, and not.

This button is used
to put text together.

Here's where
you see your
expression.

These four are also
"logical operators,"
but they're used
in modules or macros
rather than criteria.

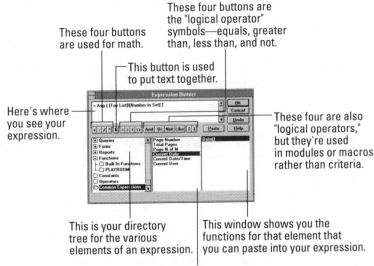

This is your directory
tree for the various
elements of an expression.

This window shows you the
functions for that element that
you can paste into your expression.

This window shows you either
the names of the elements or
the categories for functions.

The folders in the lower-left of the window contain the various elements that you can use to create your expression. You use these folders to obtain the names of the various fields and controls within your database. A folder marked with a plus (like the Forms folder in the figure) indicates that the folder contains additional folders that are not currently being displayed. In most cases, each of the main folders for forms, reports, and queries will contain two additional folders — one for objects that are currently open in their own windows and one for all the other objects in the database. To display the subfolders, simply double-click on the plus. When all of the folders are displayed, the main folder is marked with a minus (like the Functions folder in the figure).

If you are creating a criteria, the various comparisons that you can use are listed in the Operators folder (in the Comparison category). Of course, there are only seven, and it's just easier to memorize them. They're >, <, =, >=, <=, <>, and Between. When you insert an operator, the Expression Builder places «expr» markers to indicate where you need to insert the values for the criteria. The Constants folder contains some values that are useful when creating your expressions, such as the one for an empty string (= "" as a criteria means that the field is empty).

For relatively simple calculations such as *=[Number in Set] + 3* (increasing the value by three for an Update query) or *=[Last Name] & "'s " & [Shape] & "s"* (create a field with results like

Mike's Triangles), you can just use the lists of elements within the object folders and the button across the middle of the Expression Builder. There are three additional mathematical operators available within the Operators folder: ^ (for exponents or raising a number to a power of another), \ (for returning only the integer part of the answer from a division operation), and MOD (for returning the remainder from a division operation).

For more complex calculations, such as a validation rule that a date must be within the past thirty days *(<=Date() - 30)*, you need to use the built-in functions. To see the list of functions, select the Built-In folder and then select a category from the middle window. (The default category is <All>, which lists every available built-in function.) The lower-right window displays a list of all of the functions in the selected category. To use a function, select the function and then click on the Paste button (or just double-click on the function). In you haven't already entered an element name or a formula for the function, Access will add an «expr» marker to remind you. To find out more about a function, select the function and click on the Help button.

Access has a set of predefined text fields in the Common Expressions folder. These include the current date, the current page, and the total number of pages in a report or form.

More stuff

 You can also use the Expression Builder to create controls that calculate a value in a report or a form. Open the control's property sheet (using View➪Properties) and the click on the button to the left of the Control Source property. With this feature, you can create a text box in the header for your report that says something like "Page 15 of 417." The formula to do this is in the Contents folder and is identified as "Page N of M."

 The AND and OR operators are intended for use with macros or modules. To create a criteria using an OR, put each part of the statement on a separate criteria line. An AND is represented by putting each part of the statement on the same line. (See Query➪Select for a more detailed explanation.) The EQV, IMP, and XOR operators can be found in the Operators folder in the Expression builder.

 Where you are determines what you get when you click on the Build button. If you're changing the Data Source property for a form or report, you'll get the Query Builder. If you're designing a table, the Build button on the toolbar will give you the Field Builder. If you're on the Input Mask property for a field (when designing a table), clicking on the Build button to the right of the text box opens the Input Mask Wizard.

For a quick introduction to the query screen (which is basically the Query Builder), see Query⇨Select.

Chapter 4 of *Access 2 For Dummies* covers using the Table Wizard and the list of predefined fields.

File⇨Add-ins

Controls what special tools (like the Add-in Manager) are available from within Access. In general, you won't have to use this command. If you don't recognize any of the names in the submenu, don't bother with them. No matter where you are, you can get to this command.

Just the facts

When you select File⇨Add-ins, Access displays a list (similar to the following figure) of all the available add-ins.

An add-in is a special tool that isn't really part of the Access program but works together with Access to perform a task. For most users, the most useful standard add-in is the Database Documentor. This tool goes through your database and collects information to show how your database is constructed. Although you can accomplish the same thing by moving through your database and using the Print Definition command, it's much easier to use the Documentor. This tool is pretty straightforward, and the best way to see how it works is to give it a try. It's perfectly safe so feel free to experiment.

Another useful tool, the Import Database, allows you to bring in all of the objects that you created for another Access database. You can import the tables (with their data), forms, reports, and other neat stuff. When you select this add-in, you get a dialog box that enables you to select the database that you want to bring into the current database. If you just want to bring some, but not all, of the objects, see File⇨Import.

The other add-ins serve much more limited functions. Attachment Manager notifies Access when you've changed the name or location of an attached table (see File⇨Attach Table for a description of this feature). Menu Builder helps you design your own menus for use with your macros or modules. It can also be used to design a new menu structure using the Access commands, but it's best leave such changes to Microsoft. Finally, there is the Add-in Manager, which, oddly enough, manages which add-in products are available. If you get a wonderful new tool designed to work within Access, you'll use the Add-in Manager to add the tool to the Add-ins submenu.

File⇨*Attach Table*

Attaches a database table from another program to the current database. This command is useful when you already have a table that contains the information you need but was designed in another product. Access handles reading the information without bothering you with the details. You can also use this command to share a table between two Access databases. You create the table in one and then attach it in the second.

For mouse maniacs

 The Attach Table button opens the Attach dialog box, which lets you pick database tables to add to your current database.

Just the facts

Access recognizes tables created by Paradox, FoxPro, dBASE III, dBASE IV, Btrieve, or Access itself, as well as those managed by a SQL server. All of these applications work the same way — you're just using the data from a different format.

When you select the File⇨Attach Table command, you are asked to select the proper format from a list. Once you do, you're given a dialog box that allows you to move around on you're system until you find the right file. Access treats the attached table just like a regular member of the database — you can use the information in reports or forms, ask questions with queries, or edit the data itself.

More stuff

 When you're working with an SQL database, you generally need a password to gain access to the system that contains the actual data. Any changes in the structure of the SQL database or in your password on that system will break the attachment and you will have to reattach the table using File⇨Attach Table. If you can, get someone else to set up the connection for you.

 If the location or name of an external table changes, you need to use the Attachment Manager (located on the File⇨Add-ins submenu) to let Access know about the change.

If you want to change a data file created in another program to an Access format (which gives better performance), use File⇨ Import. If you want to convert an old Access 1.x table for use with Access 2.0, see File⇨Convert Database. If you're defining relationships between tables that are already part of the database, you need to use Relationships⇨Add Table. Use File⇨New (Table) to create a new table.

File⇨Close

Closes the current window (whether it's a form, report, table, or whatever). The contents of the window are saved as part of the database.

For mouse maniacs

Double-click in the Document Control box to close the current object. The bar in this box is slightly smaller than the one for the program. Double-clicking the Program Control box exits Access.

The Close Window button is only available when you are looking at a document preview. You only have to click this button once to close the current window.

For keyboard krazies

You can also use Ctrl+W, which is the Close command from the control menu.

Just the facts

An amazingly easy-to-use command. The only thing that might happen is that if you try to close a window for a report, form, or query where you haven't saved your changes, you'll be asked about whether or not to save them. If you want to keep the changes, click on Yes. If you want to throw them out (and go back to what you had when you last saved), select No.

More stuff

If you want to close everything associated with the database, go to the Database window (Window⇨Database: *Name*) and then use File⇨Close Database.

File⇨Close Database

Closes the database and any open parts (such as forms or reports). Any time you're at a Database window, this command is available for you. At other times, the command is just File⇨Close (and it only closes the current window).

For mouse maniacs

Double-click in the Document Control box on the Database window to close the database. The bar in the Document Control box is slightly smaller than the one for the Program Control box . Double-clicking the Program Control box exits Access, and double-clicking on the Document Control box for other windows just closes that window.

For keyboard krazies

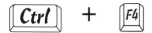

Just the facts

What could be simpler, select File⇨Close Database and Access closes up the database and all of its object windows. You are asked about saving any changes in the object windows before they are closed.

More stuff

You can only have one Access database open at a time, so it seems like it's necessary to close your old one before moving on to your next project. Not really true, because when you try to open a second database, Access closes the first.

If you just want to close an individual window, go to that window (see Window⇨*List of open objects*) and use File⇨Close.

File⇨Compact Database

Organizes the information in your database for more efficient retrieval. The database must be closed and you must have enough room for a second, temporary copy of the database. The advantage of this feature is that the new database will take up less room and may be a little faster. This is one of those strange commands that is only available when you don't have a database open.

Just the facts

The database that you want to compact needs to be closed. After you select the command, you are asked to identify which database you want to compact. (The dialog box is labeled Database To Compact From.) After you've selected the database, you need to tell Access where to put the new, compacted database. (This dialog box is labeled Database To Compact To. Original, ain't they?) Although you can specify a new name here, it's generally better to use the same one. Don't worry — Access makes sure that it has a complete, temporary copy before it begins to overwrite the original.

More stuff

It's a very, very, very good idea to backup your database before you compact it. The easiest way make a backup is to use the File Manager.

If you don't have enough room on your disk for a second copy, the whole thing will just stop. You'll have to delete some other files to make room. Consult your handy copy of *DOS For Dummies, 2nd Edition,* for more information.

When you compact your database, you have to give Access a name for the second (compacted) copy. You can either use the same name as the original or a different name. If you use a different name, you end up with two databases (one compacted and one not). Why bother? Use the same name.

File⇨Conver_t_ Database

Brings a version 1.x database up to speed for Access 2.0. The only reason that you wouldn't want to use this command is if someone who only has Access 1.x needs to use the database. This command is only available when you don't have a database open.

Just the facts

You simply select the command and identify the file that contains the database. Next, you need to give the database a new name. Access takes care of the rest. After Access has done its thing, you can generally go ahead and delete the original file.

More stuff

 If you are working in a multiuser environment (in other words, more than just you uses the database), you need to be the owner of the database to convert it, and you need to make sure that no one else is using it while you are converting.

 The Convert Database command is a one-shot deal. After you've converted an old Access database to the version 2 format, there is no easy way to change it back to a version 1.x format. If you think that you may need to use the database in the older format, keep the old version.

 If you have a database that is attached to another, you need to first convert both of them and then use File⇨Attach Table to reattach them.

File⇨Encrypt/Decrypt Database

Scrambles the information in your database so that you can only read it from within Access. Normally, you can look at a database file in a text editor or word processor and get some idea of what information it contains. For the paranoid among us, this command, combined with those on the Security menu, offer the ultimate in Access security. You may notice some loss of performance (in other words, things work slower) when you encrypt a database. This command is only available when you don't have a database open.

Just the facts

When you first select File⇨Encrypt/Decrypt Database, you have to identify the file that you want to encrypt and then, in a different dialog box, tell Access what name the file should have after it's encrypted. If you give the file a new name, you need to remember to get rid of your original, unencrypted database. Otherwise, people could just look at the original to find out all your secrets.

More stuff

 To decrypt a database, simply select it in the first dialog box. Access will recognize it as encrypted and assumes that you want to decrypt it.

 The commands on the Security menu are a better choice for limiting access, so take a look at all those commands that start with Security⇨.

File⇨Exit

Closes up everything (including the actual program) so that you can go home for the day. If you've made changes other than to the contents of the database, you'll be asked whether or not you want to save them. Content changes are saved automatically.

For mouse maniacs

 Double-click the control menu with the bigger bar to exit Access. It's the one in the far upper-right corner.

For keyboard krazies

Just the facts

Select File⇨Exit and Access starts closing down business. If you've made any changes that you haven't saved, you're given a chance to save before Access closes the window with the changes.

More stuff

 If you just want to close part of a database (such as a form or report), use File⇨Close. If you want to close a database, but not the program, go to the Database window and use File⇨Close Database.

File⇨Export

Saves a copy of the data for use with another database or spreadsheet program. You get to choose what program from a list. If your program's not on the list, you'll need to use File⇨Imp/Exp Setup.

For mouse maniacs

 Click on the Export button and your database is sent to South America with all of the appropriate custom forms already completed. (OK, the button really just changes the file format.)

Just the facts

You need to be in the database that contains the information that you want to export. After you select File⇨Export, Access presents you with the Export dialog box, which is where you identify which type of file you are trying to create.

After you've determined what it is you are creating, you need to tell Access which data you want put into the new format. You provide this information in a different dialog box that lists all the tables and queries in the current database. Next, give Access a name for the new file. Remember, you're working with files, so you're restricted to a maximum of eight letters; Access will supply the proper extension. For some formats, you are then presented with a dialog box asking you to specify the formatting options. I suggest trying it once with the default settings. If the default settings don't work to your satisfaction, you may need to get a guru to help you fine-tune the format. Don't worry about trying the export several times because your original database is left untouched.

More stuff

If you want to have control over the format of what's in the file, you need to use File⇨Output To, which can output forms, reports, and tables.

File⇨Imp/Exp Setup

Lets you define the format for an import or export operation. Most of these operations are very painful and it's much better if you can get someone else to do them. If you have to do them yourself, make sure that you have all the answers for the questions on the dialog box. Fortunately, you save your setup just in case you ever have to do it again.

Just the facts

File⇨Imp/Exp Setup is sort of a last resort when you can't get File⇨Export (or File⇨Import) to work. After you select the command, you see the following dialog box in which you can tell Access how to do its job.

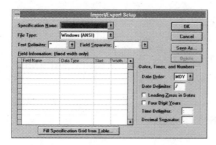

If you want to start by modifying an existing definition, just select from the Specification Name list. The next step is to decide on the file format. If you're working with another Windows program, then Windows (ANSI) is probably the best choice. You then need to specify settings in *either* the Text Delimiter area (what you want around text information) and the Field Separator area (what you want between the fields) *or* the Field Information area (how you want each column, or field, labeled and organized). If you're using information that's associated with a table already in your database, you can use the Fill Specification Grid From Table button to use that table's format to fill in the field information.

On the lower-left side of the dialog box is a group of controls called Dates, Times, and Numbers. These buttons control the formatting of (surprise!) dates, times, and numbers. For most situations, Access will have used the right information based upon how you set up Windows. The only time you really need to change these controls is if you're sending your file to someone who uses a different format (such as commas instead of periods in numbers).

After you've have everything the way you want it, you need to save your settings. If you are changing a definition, you can just choose to replace the old one by clicking on OK. If you want to create a new definition, select Save As, type in a name, and then click OK. To actually use your definition, you need to use either File⇨Import or File⇨Export.

More stuff

You can also get to the Imp/Exp dialog box by selecting the Edit Spec button in the Import Text Options dialog box while using File⇨Import.

If you just want to use a file of data created for another program, try File⇨Attach Table. If you want to use the data from your table with another program, check File⇨Output To, which may be more of what you had in mind. Before you get involved in defining a setup, check whether your desired format is on the list for File⇨Import or File⇨Export.

File⇨Import

Changes a data file from another format into the one used by Access 2.0. The list of choices is shown in the figure for "Just the facts" in File⇨Export. If your program's not on the list, you'll need to use File⇨Imp/Exp Setup to create a definition. Any time you're at a Database window, this command is available.

For mouse maniacs

 Click on the Import button and that South American database will be brought right on into your Access community.

Just the facts

The first step is to select the type of file that your trying to bring into the current database. Fortunately, you get to pick from a list. Next, pick the file that you're trying to bring in using a dialog box that enables you to tour over your hard disk. Depending upon what type of file you're working with, you have some options regarding how Access proceeds. With all file types, you can choose between the Create New Table or the Append To Existing Table options.

After Access has read the file and inserted as much data as it can, it generates a special table called Import Errors. Access will notify you if there are any errors reported. If it looks as if most of the data was imported successfully, you can print out a copy of the table and make corrections to the data in Access. If Access finds a great deal of errors (particularly many of the same kind of errors), you may want to try to fix the problem in your original file or change the options that you picked in the last step of importing.

More stuff

 One of the most common types of errors is trying to fit the wrong type of data into a field. No matter how many times you ask, Access will not put letters into a number field. You need to change the field type within your Access table. If you can't figure out what's wrong, try importing into a new table and look at how Access defines the fields.

 If you just want to use the data file (without changing its format), you can probably use File⇨Attach Table to add it to an Access database.

File⇨List of recent files

Lists your four most recently used databases so that you can open them quickly. The database that you used last will always be first. This command is only available when you don't have a database opened.

Just the facts

The very fact that the most recently used commands are on the File menu is one of the most useful shortcuts in existence (particularly for authors who have to revise the same file over and over again). Alt, F, 1 opens the file used last — that is, the first one on the list.)

More stuff

If you work with the same database all the time, it's position on the list should stay the same. However, if you work with a variety of databases (more than four), the names on the list and their positions may change.

If your database isn't on the list, you'll need to use File⇨Open Database.

File⇨Load From Query

Lets you use a saved query as a filter. The advantage to this feature is that a filter only limits what you're viewing. A query actually creates a subset of the data (and may take longer). Of course, to use the command, you have to be creating a filter (by using Records⇨Edit Filter/Sort).

Just the facts

Make sure that you've saved a query before you try to use it. This command brings a query definition in for use as a filter.

More stuff

You need to use File⇨Save As Query in order to store a filter as a query.

For information about working with queries, see Chapter 9 of *Access 2 For Dummies*.

Creates a new object for your database (such as a table, form, or report). This command is the starting point for getting to most of the Access Wizards.

The long keyboard way to select one of these command variations is to pick from the File➪New submenu. The long mouse way to use this command is to go to the Database window, click on the tab that represents what you want to create, and then click on the New button. For more information about this method of using the Database window, see its entry.

For creating forms

 The New Form button appears when you are viewing or designing a table, form, or query. It lets you choose between creating a blank form or using the Form Wizard (see the next button).

 You get the Form Wizard button on the dialog box for creating a new form. Click this button to start the Form Wizard. You can then pick the type of form to create. (The button on the right in the New Form dialog box lets you create a blank form.)

 Using the AutoForm button is the fastest way to generate a very basic form when you're looking at your data (whether as a table, form, or query results). Clicking this button immediately starts the Wizard used for creating new, single-column forms and uses the fields in the current Table or Query results.

For creating queries

 The New Query button appears when you are viewing or designing a table, form, or query. It lets you choose between creating a query with or without the Form Wizard (see the next button).

 You get the Query Wizard button on the dialog box for creating a new query. The button that appears on your screen to the right of this one (after you do the File➪New➪Query thing) lets you create a new, blank Query.

For creating reports

 The New Report button appears when you are viewing or designing a table, form, or query. It lets you choose between creating a blank report or using the Report Wizard (see the next button).

 You get the Report Wizard button on the dialog box for creating a new report. Click this button to start the Report Wizard. You then can pick the type of report to create. (The button on the right in the New Report dialog box lets you create a blank report.)

The AutoReport button is the fastest way to generate a quick report when you're looking at your data (whether as a table, form, or query results). It immediately starts the Wizard used for creating new single-column reports and uses the fields in the current Table or Query results.

For creating tables

Use the Table Wizard button to create a new table. Click this button to start the Table Wizard. You then can pick the type of table to create. (The button on the right in the New Table dialog box lets you create a blank table.)

Just the facts

Once the New submenu is displayed (File⇨New), you can select the type of object to create from the submenu.

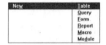

Selecting from the New submenu is the same as selecting a tab and the New button on the Database window. In either case, when creating a table, form, report, or query, you are presented with a dialog box offering a choice between using a Wizard and creating the object from scratch. Although Wizards guide you through the basic steps, their results aren't very sophisticated when it comes to reports or forms. Furthermore, it's often much easier to go around the Wizard (by selecting the Blank option).

More stuff

If you already have a form, report, or query that is close to what you want, you don't have to start from scratch to create your new one. Instead, open the one closest to what you need and then use File⇨Save As to make a copy with a different name.

If you want a whole new database, you need to be at the Database window when you choose File⇨New Database. See the Database window section for a discussion of creating new objects that way.

File⇨New Database

Starts a brand-new, empty database. In the perfect world, someone else would design all of your databases and you'd just use them. This command is available when you don't have a database open or from any Database window.

For mouse maniacs

 Click the New Database button to win a new, blank Database window to fill with your own tables, reports, forms, and other doodads.

For keyboard krazies

Just the facts

The only thing you really have to keep in mind is that because Access saves the database as a file, you need to restrict yourself to eight characters maximum as the name. Other than that, you just select the command and type the new name. You have to give the name at the start because Access saves your work automatically as you go.

More stuff

 If you just want a new object for your database (like a form or report), you should be looking at File⇨New.

 See Chapter 2 of *Access 2 For Dummies*.

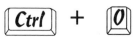 **File⇨Open Database**

Opens any Access database for you. What you end up with is the Database window for that database. You can then use it to open whatever part you need to work with (a table, form, report, or whatever).

For mouse maniacs

 It's a good thing these buttons don't wear out because you'll use the Open button every time you change databases (unless the name of the database that you want to open already appears on the File menu).

For keyboard krazies

Just the facts

The only possible problem with this command is remembering where you stored the database. When you select File⇨Open Database, you're presented with a dialog box that lets you move around on your hard disk. After you locate the database file that you want, simply double-click on it to load it into Access and open the Database window.

More stuff

It's faster to use the File⇨*List of recent files* if your database is listed there. If you want a new database, you need either to be at a Database window or to not have any database open; you then use File⇨New Database. Where Access looks first to open a database is an option that you can set with View⇨Options.

File⇨Output To

Creates a copy of your data organized in the format that you request (if you ask nicely). This command has shortcuts for working with Excel or Word. (Oddly enough, both of these applications are also Microsoft products.)

For mouse maniacs

 You should probably only use the Output To Excel button if you have access to Excel. This button is available when you're at the Database window or previewing your output.

 Use the Output To Word button when you want to take your report into Word for some fine-tuning. This little button is available when you are previewing your output.

 Rev up the mail merge process with the Mail Merge Wizard button, which is available only at the Database window.

Just the facts

If you're not using one of the shortcut buttons, select File⇨Output To; you'll get the Output To dialog box.

The options on the menu are pretty easy to figure out. You've got your basic Excel format; your very, very basic text format (quite

boring); and the nerdy Rich Text Format (RTF). RTF is the best
choice for preserving all of the formatting of your report, but it is
really designed for use with word processors. If you're trying to
use another spreadsheet program, use the Excel format. Even if
you don't have Excel, most other spreadsheets can read the format.
MS-DOS Text is a last resort; it gets rid of any fancy formatting.

More stuff

 If you are going to be moving information into a spreadsheet, you
probably want to organize your report into columns — the closest
layout to the spreadsheet grid. If you're going into a word processor, you can be as creative as you want — the word processor
can probably handle it. If you want to use your data for a mail
merge, you should be at the Database window and not in a report.

 The way Access works with Word is a little bit confusing. The
Output To Word button actually creates the Word file based upon
the format of the report. The Mail Merge Wizard only works with
Microsoft Word for Windows 6 and is the best choice for creating
form letters. It opens a Wizard that guides you through the
process of merging your data with a Word document.

 If you want to use all of the data in your database with another
program, you may be better off using the File⇨Export command.

 To really get the power out of Access in the typical business office,
you'll want to learn everything in Chapter 21 and Chapter 22 of
Access 2 For Dummies. These chapters show you how to do a variety
of fancy things with your data without resorting to using Word.

File⇨*Print*

Produces a printout of what you're working with in whatever
format you are currently using. In other words, if you are viewing
your data in a form, printing will create a copy of that form for
each record. If you are using a report, your records will be
formatted to fit into the report. You can also use File⇨Print to
create a file containing the information for printing later.

For mouse maniacs

 It's not available when you are designing things, but click on the
Print button to print a copy of whatever information you are
currently viewing using your normal printing options.

For keyboard krazies

 +

Just the facts

If you just want to print one copy of whatever you are looking at, you can generally just select the File⇨Print command and then press Enter (or click OK). Otherwise, you're free to change the various options.

More stuff

If you want to print only a portion of what you're working with, you can try two approaches. If you enter a range on the Print dialog, Access assumes that you mean the actual pages in the output. If you want a specific group of records in a form or datasheet, select those records before selecting File⇨Print. In the Print dialog, select Print Selection. Access will format the output so that the first selected record is treated as the first record for the form or table.

To control the way Access uses your printer, use File⇨Print Setup. If you want a printout summarizing how your database is organized (or the format of a particular report), use File⇨Print Definition instead.

Chapter 16 of *Access 2 For Dummies* covers printing information in a report.

File⇨Print Definition

Gives you a copy of the information regarding how things within your database are organized. In most case, what you get is a listing of the properties of all of the controls within the object (generally a report or form).

Just the facts

This command is primarily used for documenting your database. What you get depends upon which type of object you have selected before you use the command. This command is most useful for forms and reports for which you can get a printout showing how each control works. In addition to documentation, the definitions are also useful for tracking down strange problems or for making sure that everything is consistent, which is particularly helpful if you are working with macros or complex controls on forms.

More stuff

If you want to print out the contents of your database, you need to use File⇨Print. If you want to completely document your database, you can use the Database Documentor found on the File⇨Add-ins submenu.

File⇨Print Preview

Shows you what your output is going to look like. Print Preview formats the information based upon what you are viewing (a table, form, or report) and the settings in Print Setup. It's usually a good idea to preview your work before printing, as reports may be many pages long, and you don't want to waste that much paper.

For mouse maniacs

 Click on the Print Preview button to see what you would be printing if you'd selected the Print command instead.

 The Zoom button shows you the finer details when you're previewing your work. You can't make any changes, but this button lets you make sure that everything is really the way you want it.

For keyboard krazies

The Z shortcut zooms the view of your document, but *only* when you are in Print Preview.

Just the facts

When you select Print Preview, Access prepares a screen copy of your final output. You can move through the document to check that everything looks OK. Not only does this feature save paper, but you can use the various tools to correct mistakes while you view the output.

More stuff

 How closely the preview matches your output is determined primarily by two factors — how good your screen is and how good your printer is. It's not too amazing to find out that the more you spent on your equipment, the better it works. A standard VGA monitor with either an ink-jet or laser printer gives a close enough match for most people. The other problem that you may run into involves the fonts that you use. Stick with those that have a double T to the left in the fonts list and you should be fine.

 You need to use File⇨Print to actually get your results. If you are working with a report, it's faster to use File⇨Sample Preview.

 Everything you need to know about printing is in Chapter 16 of *Access 2 For Dummies.*

File⇨Print Setup

Controls how Access uses your printer and, if you have more than one, which printer Access uses. You can control the margins, the printer resolution, and the orientation of the text on the paper.

For mouse maniacs

 You need to be previewing your document via the Print Preview command to use the Print Setup button.

For keyboard krazies

But *only* if you are previewing your document with Print Preview or Sample Preview.

Just the facts

There are four issues to consider with Print Setup. First, you have to choose a printer. Second, you have to decide on your margins. The margins are the amount of nonprinting space on the edge of each page. Wider margins make for better looking output while narrow margins fit more onto the page. Third, you have to choose an orientation, either portrait or landscape. Finally, you have to choose the paper size that you are using in your printer.

Access saves the information in Print Setup separately for each report and form, so you usually only have to worry about getting things right the first time. After that, the settings should probably stay the same — at least until you buy that new laser printer you've been eyeing.

More stuff

 The Print Setup command is also available from the button of the same name on the Print dialog box. So you end up getting there by using File⇨Print and clicking the Setup button.

 Use File⇨Print Preview to get an idea of what you'll get when you finally print. If you're working with a report, use File⇨Sample Preview to get a faster preview. You use File⇨Print to actually print your report.

 Everything you need to know about printing is in Chapter 16 of *Access 2 For Dummies*.

File⇨Rename

Changes the names to protect the innocent. As you might expect, you use this command to change object names. You can use spaces in your names, and you can use up to 64 characters, but spaces count as characters.

Just the facts

You won't find any shortcuts for this command. The command is, however, very simple to use. You simply select the object that you want to rename, select File⇨Rename, and type in the new name.

More stuff

You can rename tables belonging to other programs that you are using with the File⇨Attach Table command. The tables keep their old names for the program that created them; the longer name is only used within Access.

File⇨Repair Database

Makes things all better after an accident that damages your database. This is one of those commands that you hope you never have to use. Fortunately, if you do need it, you don't have a lot of choices as to how to use it. This command is only available when you don't have a database opened.

Just the facts

You need to close the damaged database and be at the Database window to use this command. If Access detects a problem with a database, it will automatically try to run Repair. That's fine. Go ahead and let it. If a database starts behaving strangely (boy, that's a technical definition for you), you may want to try running Repair to see if the problem clears up. Common problems: Access is unable to find a record even though you know its in the database (often you're staring right at the record when Access says it's not there), or Access fails to update a record correctly when you change views.

File⇨Run Macro

Actually makes a macro do whatever it is suppose to. A *macro* is a recorded series of instructions, and this command tells Access to execute those instructions.

For mouse maniacs

 Be careful though. On the Query Design screen, this button runs the query, not a macro. If you use a macro often, it's easier to assign the macro to its own button using the View⇨Toolbars⇨Customize option.

Just the facts

There are a number of ways to run a macro, but this command is generally the easiest (unless you assign the macro a shortcut). To use most of the methods, you need to know the macro's name (though not how it works). If you're at the Database window, you can select the Macro tab, select the macro from the list and then click on the Run button. Everywhere else (except when editing macros, which I'm NOT going to talk about), you need to select File⇨Run Macro and then the name of the macro. If you know the name, you can type it in directly rather than selecting it from the list.

More stuff

 You may want to look at *PC World Microsoft Access 2 Bible, 2nd Edition* for some help with macros.

File⇨Sample Preview

Shows your report with enough of your information to get an idea of what the final draft will look like. This command is a fast preview that just grabs records (ignoring any selection rules) and tries to put the records into the groups on your report so that you can see the layout. This command is only available when you are designing a report.

For mouse maniacs

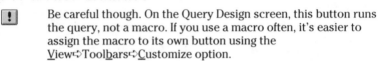 Click the Sample Report button for a quick look at what you've been creating.

Just the facts

Keep in mind that when you use Sample Preview, the records are not complete. You can't trust any of the values that appear on screen when you are previewing a sample.

More stuff

To actually see what your report will look like with the proper data, you need to use File⇨Print Preview.

File⇨Save

Takes whatever design you are working with (a table, report, form, or query) and saves it under the current name. If you are looking at a datasheet, the command name changes to remind you what it is you are saving (a form, query, or table).

For mouse maniacs

The Save button is one of the most popular buttons on any toolbar.

For keyboard krazies

Shift + F12

Ctrl + S

Just the facts

You just need to select the Save command to save any new information. If you haven't saved the material before, you'll have to provide a name for the new object. Remember that you can use up to 64 characters, and you can include spaces. After you name an object, selecting File⇨Save will just store the changes without pausing to ask for a name.

More stuff

If you try to close an object that you've changed, you'll be asked about saving the changes. If you've already named the object, clicking Yes will save the changes. If you haven't saved it before, after you click Yes, you'll have to give the object a name.

Designs are saved as part of the database. There is no way to save the design of an object separately from the database. You can use a design to organize the information that you are saving by using File⇨Output To.

If you want to change the name of what you are working with (or you want to make a copy), then use File⇨Save As. If you want to create a separate file containing the information (rather than the design), you need to use File⇨Output To. If you want a record of a design, you need to use File⇨Print Definition.

File⇨Save As

Creates a new copy of whatever you are working on under a new name. If you specify the same name, the old copy is replaced, but then you could have used File⇨Save instead. You need to use this command when you want a copy under a new name. Like the Save command, if you are at a datasheet, the command name changes to remind you of what you are saving. You use the Save As command when you are designing your own tables, forms, reports, or queries. The command changes to Save Form As and Save Query As when you are working with forms and queries respectively. (No duh!)

Just the facts

Use this command only when you want to create a copy of the current object under a new name. After you select the command, you'll be asked to name the object.

More stuff

You will often use this command when you have a form or report that you are going to use as a starting point for something else. You don't want to change your original because you still need that format, so you open it and make a copy under a new name with Save As. Because it doesn't make any sense to have two tables with similar designs, there is no File⇨Save As command when working with tables.

If you start with an existing object (call it First Form), make changes, and then use Save As with a new name (Second Form), then the original remains unchanged, and the changes are only in the second copy (Second Form).

They may sound similar, but the File⇨Save As Query and File⇨Save As Report commands are very different. They change the format of what you are working with. If you want to save a copy of the contents of your database, you need to use File⇨Output To.

File⇨Save As Query

Converts a filter into a query. You need to save in this way because you can't save a filter.

Just the facts

Occasionally, you'll design a filter for selecting information and decide that it's a search that you need to do fairly often. Rather than recreate the filter each time, you can just save it as a query for later use. Simply select File⇨Save As Query and then give the newly created query a name.

More stuff

 To use the query as a filter, you need to use File⇨Load From Query. Note that Save As and Save As Query are different commands.

File⇨Save As Report

Makes a copy of a form into a report. Because both reports and forms are created with the same tools, you may find it easier to modify an existing form when making a new report. Or you may have started working in a form design before you realized that what you really wanted was a report. This command is only available when you are designing a form.

Just the facts

There are no shortcuts for this command. After all, you should have started with a report if that was what you wanted. After you select the command, you just need to give the new report a name.

More stuff

 If you want to keep a copy of the form with your changes, select File⇨Save (or File⇨Save Form depending upon which view you are using) before using File⇨Save As Report.

File⇨Save Layout

Stores any changes that you have made to the display of the relationships between tables in your database. This command sets what you'll see when you open the relationships display. You use this command when you are working with the relationships (links) between the tables in your database.

Just the facts

Selecting Save Layout sets the view that you get when you select Edit⇨Relationships. It doesn't change the actual relationships, and you can use the commands on the Relationship menu to change the view at any time. Just be sure that you are happy with the way you are displaying the relationships in the window before selecting Save Layout.

More stuff

It's generally more desirable to set the standard layout to include all of the related tables in your database. That way, when you open the Layout window (with Edit⇨Relationships), you get a bird's-eye view over your entire structure. If you want to look at a more focused view, just use Edit⇨Clear Grid and start with a fresh layout.

To create a record of the existing relationships, use File⇨Print Definition from the Layout window. If you want to start over designing the relationships, use Edit⇨Clear Layout.

See Chapter 18 of *Access 2 For Dummies*.

File⇨Save Record

Forces Access to save any changes that you made to the current record. Even though Access saves every time you move between records, it's still nice to be able to make sure that Access saved what you just did. You use this command whenever you are looking at your data either as a table or in a form.

For keyboard krazies

Shift + **Enter**

Just the facts

Selecting File⇨Save Record forces Access to immediately save any changes that you have made to the current record. Access will automatically save the changes when you move away from the record (to another record), but this command let's you force the save in case you just want to sit and stare at the record for awhile.

More stuff

Of course, if you didn't mean to make those changes, you may want to look at Edit⇨Undo and Edit⇨Undo Current Field/Record.

File⇨Send

Works only if you are on a network and have e-mail. If you do, this command sends a copy of what you are working on out to someone else. It works just like Print except without the paper.

For mouse maniacs

If you're previewing your document and have Microsoft Mail, you can send your document on its way with a single click of the Send Mail button.

Just the facts

File⇨Send bundles up the current object and sends it via your electronic mail system. After selecting the command, you are presented with a dialog box where you can select who you want to receive the message and, depending upon your mail system, set other features such as sending duplicate copies. Most importantly, you will need to specify a file format for the message. Which one you select depends, in part, on what programs the other person has available.

More stuff

Use File⇨Print Preview to make sure that you are sending the information that you want in a format that the other person will be able to understand. There's nothing more frustrating than junk mail!

See File⇨Output To for more information about possible file formats.

Format⇨Align

Lines up the selected control. This command helps you make your forms and reports look much neater. The command doesn't say *Align Controls*, but it should.

Just the facts

Format⇨Align is a bit too complex to have a shortcut. First, you must select the object (or objects if you want to line up more than one). Next, you select the Align command and you'll see the Align submenu:

The only control that is available on the submenu when you have a single control selected is To Grid. Selecting To Grid moves the control so that the upper-left corner is aligned with the grid. To get the same results automatically when you create or move a control, activate Format⇨Snap to Grid.

With multiple controls selected, you can choose which side to align the controls (left, right, top, or bottom). You will generally want to align the controls to a side and then use a spacing command to spread them out evenly. You use Format⇨Vertical Spacing if you've aligned the left or right side and Format⇨Horizontal Spacing if you've aligned the top or bottom.

More stuff

If you want to make a group of controls the same size, see Format⇨Size. If you want to change the way text is formatted within fields, see the entry under Format⇨*Text for Controls*. In reality, all of those commands are buttons, but I made up entries so that you can find them.

Format⇨Apply Default

Quickly changes the selected control's characteristics to match the default (a group of settings that you decided upon). Each control has its own default settings which are stored separately.

Just the facts

Select the control or controls that you want to change in a form design and then select the command. Each control will be changed to the default format for that type of control.

More stuff

If you select a group of mixed controls (a couple of check boxes and a few radio buttons), when you select Format⇨Apply Default, each type of control is adjusted separately. This side-effect results from the fact that you need to set the default for each type of control independently.

 To find out the default settings for a control, select the tool used to create the control (from the toolbox) and then View↪Properties. If you want, you can change the properties directly on the tool's property sheet, but it's generally easier to use Format↪Change Default.

Format↪Bring to Front

Moves the selected control to the top layer of the report or form. Controls that are on top can cover up controls on the bottom.

Just the facts

Although this command will work with a group of controls, it's generally used by selecting a single control (by clicking on it once) and then selecting the command.

More stuff

 Just because you can't see a control doesn't mean it doesn't exist. If you've moved a larger control to the front, you may have covered up other controls. Try sending things to the back until you find the control that you misplaced.

 If you select a group of controls, the entire group is moved, but the layers within the group remain the same. Selecting a group of controls can be helpful when working with a set of grouped controls. In that case, try to always move the controls as a group.

 The opposite command, Format↪Send To Back, is sometimes more useful because it doesn't cover things up as you work.

Format↪Change Default

Stores the default settings for a type of control in a form design. With this command (and the help of Format↪Apply Default), you can easily create a series of controls with the same look by changing the format of the other controls to match.

Just the facts

The first step in using this command is to format a control in the way that you want it to look. You do this task by using the features

available on the Palette (see View⇨Palette) and the Format menu.
After the control looks the way you want, click on it once and
then select Format⇨Change Default. Now, you're all set to move
to another control and format it to match by selecting it and then
choosing Format⇨Apply Default.

More stuff

Access stores default settings on the property sheet of the tool
used to create the control. If you want, you can select the tool
and use View⇨Properties to view the property sheet and make
changes. When you're familiar with the commands for formatting
a control, most of the entries on the various controls' property
sheets are self-explanatory.

This command works together with Format⇨Apply Default. You
need to use the controls on the Palette and toolbox to change the
look of a control (see View⇨Palette and View⇨Toolbox).

See Chapter 14 of *Access 2 For Dummies*.

Format⇨Column Width

Changes the width of a column or group of columns. When
viewing a datasheet (as a table or the results of a query) or
designing a table, this command is available.

For mouse maniacs

✛ You need to be at the right edge of the column to use the Column
Resize cursor.

`Best Fit` The Best Fit button is on the Column Width dialog box. It adjusts
each column to the smallest possible size; the smallest size is
determined by the largest entry in the column.

Just the facts

To use this command, you can either select a single column (by
being anywhere within the column) or a group of side-by-side
columns (by dragging over the field names for the columns of the
group). Next, select Format⇨Column Width (or use the right
button menu). Finally, you have one of three options: type a
number representing the relative width for the selected
column(s); click on the Standard Width check box; or select the
Best Fit button. If you enter a number or use the Standard Width
option, all columns in a group will have same width. If you use
Best Fit, each column will be adjusted individually.

If you are using the mouse to change the column width, move your pointer until the double-headed arrow appears and then drag the column border to its new width. You can change the width for a group of columns by using the mouse. Just select the entire group first and then use the mouse to change the width for any of the columns within the group. All columns in the group will be given the new width.

More stuff

If you want to eliminate a column from a datasheet temporarily, you can use Format⇨Hide Columns.

Format⇨Font

Changes the font used for displaying text within a datasheet. The contents of all fields must be displayed in the same font.

Just the facts

It doesn't matter what you do before you select the command, as the font setting will change the entire datasheet. However, each datasheet stores its own font information, so different datasheets can use different fonts. After you select the command, you can make your selections from the lists for Font, Font Style, and Size and view the results in the Sample box in the lower-right corner.

More stuff

If you're printer supports TrueType fonts (most ink-jet and laser printers do), you should select a font with the double T to the left (indicating a TrueType font). If not, you should select one with a miniature printer to the left (indicating a printer font). If you're system prints particularly slowly with a TrueType font, you may get better performance by changing to a printer font.

If you want to change the way text is displayed in a form or report, see the entry Format⇨*Text for Controls*.

Format⇨Form Header/Footer

Controls whether the header at the start of the form and the footer at the end of the form exist. A check mark indicates that such sections exist and are on the form design screen.

Just the facts

The first time you select this command, Access adds the form header and form footer sections to your form. If you select the command again, Access gets rid of those sections and any controls that they contain. When you go to select the command, always check to see whether or not there is a check mark next to the Form Header/Footer command. If you see a check mark, then the form header and form footer are currently included, and selecting the command will delete them. When the form footer and form header exist, you can use any of the form design tools to add information to those sections.

More stuff

To set a header or footer on each page, use Format⇨Page Header/Footer.

Format⇨Freeze Columns

Positions the field (or fields) to the left of the table screen and locks them there. The scroll bar along the bottom of the screen will no longer cause these columns to move. Other columns that have not been frozen behave normally. You can freeze a series of individual columns to group them on the left.

Just the facts

This command isn't one that you want to turn on by accident, so there is no shortcut. Just select the first column (or adjacent columns) that you want to freeze and select the command. The column (or columns) move to the far left and are no longer affected by the scrolling the columns. If you want to freeze additional columns, simply follow the same steps. The newly frozen columns will be placed to the right of any previously frozen columns (but still to the left of any unfrozen columns).

More stuff

The frozen columns are actually moved to the left and remain there even after you unfreeze them, which means that every time you use the Freeze Column command, Access reorganizes your table.

If you use this command, be sure you that know about Format⇨ Unfreeze All Columns, which is the only command that unlocks the columns. Although the columns are locked into position, you can still change their width (see Format⇨Column Width).

Format➪Gridlines

Controls whether the boundaries between fields and records are marked as lines. Gridlines make it easier to see what goes where but also harder to read the actual information. A check mark next to the command means that the gridlines are being displayed. The command is on the Format menu (rather than the View menu) because it also controls whether the gridlines are included in printouts of the datasheet.

Just the facts

Each time you select this command, you either turn the display of the gridlines on or off. When you start out, Access displays them, so the first time you select Format➪Gridlines, they disappear.

Format➪Hide Columns

Temporarily removes a column from a datasheet. This feature is great when you need a quick printout of some of the information in your database but not all of it. If you are designing a table or looking at a datasheet (either a table or the results of a query), this command is available.

Just the facts

To hide a column (or columns), simply select what you want to hide and then select Format➪Hide Columns. If you want to hide a number of columns that aren't side-by-side, you may want to use Format➪Show Columns, which gives you a list of all the columns on the datasheet and lets you hide them by clicking a check box.

More stuff

You may forget that you have columns hidden and either panic because your data is missing or add another field that you don't need with duplicate information. So be careful when hiding columns.

Format➪Show Columns is a much more flexible command that not only lets you restore hidden columns but also hide new ones.

Chapter 16 of *Access 2 For Dummies* talks about hiding columns when printing a datasheet.

Format⇨Horizontal Spacing

Positions a group of controls in a form based upon the horizontal space between them. You can increase or decrease the amount of space or make it equal.

Just the facts

You select the controls and then the command. When you select Horizontal Spacing, Access displays the submenu.

The three choices are pretty clear: Increase puts more space between each pair of controls; Decrease gets rid of some of the space; and Make Equal balances the spacing between the controls. Both Increase and Decrease add a fixed amount of space each time you select the command, so to add a great deal of space, select the command several times.

More stuff

You generally want to align a group of controls before adjusting the spacing. To adjust the alignment of the controls, you need to use Format⇨Align. To control the spacing up-and-down on the screen, use Format⇨Vertical Spacing.

Format⇨Page Header/Footer

Controls whether there is a header at the top and a footer at the bottom end of each page. A check mark indicates that the page header and footer exist and are on the design screen. You'll find that this command is available when you are designing the layout for a report or form.

Just the facts

The first time you select this command, Access adds a header and footer section to your form, both of which will print at the top (head) and bottom (foot) of each page of your form. The check mark next to the command indicates that the page header and page footer are active and will be included. If you select the command again, Access removes the check mark and deletes any information in the header and footer.

More stuff

Always look for the check mark in the menu before selecting this command. If you see a check mark, then the header and footer are active even if you can't currently see them on the screen. Try scrolling up to the very top of the form to locate the header. (If you have a form header, the page header is below it.)

If you want to position a header and footer around each form, you can use Format⇨Form Header/Footer.

Format⇨Row Height

Sets the height for the rows in a datasheet. Each row represents one record. If the information in a field (column) is too wide to fit, Access will split it onto two or more lines. To see the extra lines, you need to increase the height of the entire row.

For mouse maniacs

You need to be on the bottom line of a row to use the Row Height cursor. Just drag the line to adjust the height.

Just the facts

You can only have one row height setting for all of the rows in the datasheet, so your position in a row or the selection of a row will not affect the command functions. You can either use the mouse to drag the line between rows to change the height or select Format⇨Row Height. The dialog box offers two choices: entering a value for the height or using the standard height. The standard height displays one line and is based upon the current font size.

More stuff

If you want to change the width of the fields, use Format⇨Column Width. Changing the font used in the fields (with Format⇨Font) changes the standard row height.

Format⇨Send to Back

Moves the layer containing the selected control to the back or bottom layer. Each control is on its own layer, and those that are on top (towards the front) can cover up those behind them.

For mouse maniacs

 If you do a lot of form or report design, you'll want to add the Send To Back button to a toolbar.

Just the facts

To use this command, select the control and then the command. Don't worry too much if the control disappears; you sent it behind another object. If you send a control to the back and want to see it again, you have two options: either move other controls to the back until the missing control reappears or immediately select F̲ormat⇨Bring to F̲ront (the control is still selected and will pop to the top).

More stuff

TIP The easiest way to put a group of controls in order is to select the one that you want on top and then send it to the back. Next, select the control to be on the second layer and send it to the back (behind the one you just moved). Continue this process until you've moved all the controls into the order that you want.

F̲ormat⇨S̲how Columns

Gives you a list of all of the columns in the datasheet and lets you select which ones are displayed.

Just the facts

You can actually use the Show Columns command to both hide columns and restore hidden columns. When you select this command, Access presents a dialog box with all of the columns listed.

Just select the field name for the column that you want to work with and then click on the Show or Hide button as appropriate. A check mark next to a field name means that it is included in the display. No check mark means that it is hidden. When you've made your changes, click on C̲lose and you're done. There's no shortcut for bringing back hidden columns, so Show Columns is a very useful command.

More stuff

Use Format⟹Hide Columns to hide a selected column.

Chapter 16 of *Access 2 For Dummies* talks about hiding columns when printing a datasheet.

Format⟹Size

Adjusts the size of the selected control or controls. You can use this command to make a group of controls all the same size or make a control fit tightly around its contents.

Just the facts

As with the other commands used to position controls (Format⟹Align, Format⟹Vertical Spacing, and Format⟹Horizontal Spacing), you must first select the control or controls that you want to work with. Then you select the menu command, which displays a submenu.

Only two of the options are available if you have a single control selected. The first option, To Fit, adjusts the size of the control based upon the text it contains. This option is very useful when working with captions and text fields. The second, To Grid, moves each of the four corners of the control to the grid, which is represented by the pattern of dots in the background. (When designing, even circular controls like radio buttons have corners.)

If you have more than one control selected, you can adjust them so that they are all the same size. The next two choices adjust the height of the controls in the group. The final two options adjust the width. Be careful when using the To Narrowest and To Shortest options because if you make a control too small, you won't be able to see the text.

More stuff

If you want a group of controls to be the same size, you should select both To Widest and To Tallest. To evenly distribute controls in a stack, you would then select Format⟹Horizontal Spacing (Make Equal) and Format⟹Align (Left). If the controls are in a row, use Format⇨Vertical Spacing (Make Equal) and Format⇨Align (Bottom). No matter what organization you want, always adjust the size before adjusting the spacing or alignment.

After you've sized your controls, you may want to change their positions with one of the appropriate commands: Format⇨Align, Format⇨Horizontal Spacing, or Format⇨Vertical Spacing.

Format⇨Snap to Grid

Makes controls jump to the nearest dot that represents the alignment grid. The grid is used to line up the various controls that you are using, and the Snap To Grid feature makes sure that any new control is neatly aligned.

Just the facts

Turning on Snap To Grid makes it easier to size and position controls when creating or moving them. Snap To Grid is on if there is a check mark to the left of the command name. To change the setting (turn it on if it's off or turn it off if it's on), just select the command.

More stuff

The number of dots that make up the grid is a form property. Use Edit⇨Select Form and then View⇨Properties to change the setting.

View⇨Grid controls whether the grid is actually displayed.

Format⇨Text for Controls

Formats the text within controls. I made this heading up because the text formatting is actually set with a series of buttons on the standard toolbar rather than a menu command. Each button is described below in the "For mouse maniacs" section. You'll find that these commands are available when you are designing the layout for a report or form and then only as buttons on the toolbar.

For mouse maniacs

Font List: Use this button to select the font for the control (or controls).

Font Size List: Use this button to change the size of the font. You can use the Format⇨Size (To Fit) command to scale the control to the text.

Bold: Like the other buttons for formatting text, be sure to select the box containing the text first.

Italics: One click of this button and everything in the selected control (or controls) slants to the right.

Align Left: This button aligns the text in the selected control or controls to the left.

Align Center: This button centers the text in the selected control or controls.

Align Right: This button aligns the text in the selected control or controls to the right.

Just the facts

You use all of these tools the same: select the control or controls and then use the buttons on the toolbar to change the text formatting.

The first two font options, font name and font size, are drop-down lists that allow you to select your choice. The double T next to a font name indicates that it is a TrueType font, which is the preferred option for most printers. The two font style buttons (Bold and Italic) work as toggles. A lighter shading indicates that a button is depressed (call a counselor) and the text is formatted with that style. You can format text as italic, bold, both, or neither. You can only select one of the three alignment buttons (left, center, or right).

More stuff

After you've set the text properties for a particular type of control, you can use the Format⇨Change Default and Format⇨Apply Default commands to copy the text properties (along with all of the other control properties) to other controls of the same type. The View⇨Palette and View⇨Toolbox entries cover changing the look of controls. The commands for positioning controls include Format⇨Align and Format⇨Size.

Format⇨Unfreeze All Columns

Restores the normal behavior of columns in a datasheet. In other words, if you've locked columns into position along the left edge of the datasheet, this command releases them.

Just the facts

You only use this command if you've been freezing columns. All you do is select the command and the frozen columns can now be moved. The original order of the columns is not restored, so you'll have to move them back into position by hand. To move a column, click once on the field name at the top of the column and then drag it to the new location.

More stuff

 If you want to restore the columns to their original order, simply close the table and do not save the layout changes. When you reopen the datasheet, the columns will be in their previous order. Of course, you will also lose any changes that you made since your last save to other layout features such as column width or row height. If you save the table immediately before you start freezing columns, you shouldn't have any problems.

 For more information about freezing columns, see Format⇨Freeze Columns.

Format⇨Vertical Spacing

Positions a group of controls based upon the vertical space between them. You can increase or decrease the amount of space or make it equal.

Just the facts

This command requires too much detail for a shortcut. You select the control or controls and then the command. When you select Vertical Spacing, you see the command's submenu.

Vertical Spacing	Make Equal
	Increase
	Decrease

The three choices are pretty clear: Increase puts more space between each pair of controls; Decrease gets rid of some of the space; and Make Equal balances the spacing between the controls. Both Increase and Decrease add a fixed amount of space each time you select the command, so to add a great deal of space, select the command several times.

More stuff

 If you want to position things horizontally, see Format➪Horizontal Spacing. To line controls up with each other, see Format➪Align.

Help➪About Microsoft Access

Tells you more than you probably want to know about the Access copyright information. More useful is the little System Info button in the lower-right corner. This button opens a special utility that scans your system and gathers important information that you need when you call technical support.

Just the facts

Select this command and stare at the information — which is useful in case you forget what program you are running. The one very useful bit of information on the screen is your product's serial number. You may need this number to prove to the technical support people that you actually paid for the product.

If you click on the System Info button, you'll be rewarded with the Microsoft System Info utility. It's a separate program, and because I don't have a contract to talk about it, you don't get any details. Basically, you can select a category from the list at the top and find out the details of what's on your system. This information is invaluable to nerds and valueless to anyone else.

Help➪Contents

Takes you to the table of contents for the Access help file. From there, you can follow topics throughout the hypertext system.

For keyboard krazies

If you are just staring at the screen, F1 takes you directly to the Contents page for the help file. If you are in the middle of a task, this shortcut takes you to the most appropriate entry (in the help file designer's opinion).

Just the facts

When you're at the Help contents page, you have a couple of choices. The most common approach is to browse your way through the Help system by clicking on one of the underlined, green topics. The first three are generally the most useful, but don't overlook the two at the top. Help Features gives you a quick introduction to using the Help system, and What's New focuses on the new and (hopefully) improved features of Access version 2.0.

Going back to the big three, the first, Using Microsoft Access, takes you to a series of topics that are oriented around how to do tasks. Each of the first few pages is a more focused table of contents for that topic which contains more underlined green topics that you can use to move closer to your information. Eventually you get to page that actually tells you how to do what you want.

Generally speaking, pressing F1 during the middle of a task (for example, designing a form), provides you with *context-sensitive* help. Based upon what you were doing, the Help system tries to find the most relevant topic.

Each help screen contains more underlined green topics, which you can use to move through the information. In addition, many pages include a "see also" entry at the top that opens a box containing a list of related topics. You'll also find various terms marked with a dotted underline. These words are in the Glossary, and clicking on them reveals a short definition.

More stuff

Most of the time, you can get to the topic you need faster by starting the task and then pressing F1. F1 activates context-sensitive help, which means that the Help system tries to guess what you're having problems with and moves to a related Help entry.

If you are trying to figure out what something does, see the entry for what I call Help⇨*Identify Command*. The Cue Cards feature is discussed under Help⇨Cue Cards. The Search feature is covered in the discussion of Help⇨Search.

The various Access Help systems are discussed in Chapter 6 of *Access 2 For Dummies*.

Help⇨ Cue Cards

Starts the cue card system which teaches you how to perform various common (and a couple of really strange) database tasks. The only problem is that this feature runs very slowly on some systems. Of course, if it runs slowly, then Access probably does as well.

For mouse maniacs

The Cue Cards, which you can access via the Cue Cards button, guide you through various tasks within Access. They're not nearly as much fun as IDG's *Access 2 For Dummies,* though.

Just the facts

Cue Cards are designed to work with you while you learn Access. The topics in Cue Cards are marked with a small button with an arrow (OK. It's actually a greater than sign, but use your imagination) and are generally bold text (rather than underlined green text like you see in Help). The material in Cue Cards is presented in a tutorial fashion and is read in sequence. Most pages don't list any alternative topics and just contain a Next button.

Cue Cards offer many advantages over the printed documentation, but they do take some time to get used to. The Cue Card screen stays on top of your database until you close it. You can work with your database, but you'll have to make the Cue Card window smaller and continually move it to get at what you want.

More stuff

If you're having a problem doing something, try F1 (context-sensitive help) first; it is discussed under Help⇨Contents.

The various Access Help systems are discussed in Chapter 6 of *Access 2 For Dummies.*

Help⇨ Identify Command

Takes you directly to the help topic associated with a particular command. This feature is a more useful approach if you are just trying to figure out what something is used for.

For mouse maniacs

 Click the Help button, move the pointer onto the object about which you want more information, and click.

 Although ToolTips aren't actually part of the Help system, they are very useful for identifying the purpose of a button. If ToolTips are active, holding the cursor over a button will cause the button name to appear. You can turn ToolTips on and off with the View⇨Toolbars dialog box.

For keyboard krazies

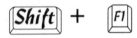

After the feature is active, you can use any keyboard shortcut to select the command that you want information on.

Just the facts

After you've activated this feature, your cursor develops a question mark at the end to remind you of what's going on. The next command that you try to use will not perform a task. Instead, after you wait a moment, the Help system will open to the topic page devoted to that menu command. (This feature also works with buttons because each button is associated with a menu command.)

More stuff

 The menu command must be available in order for you to get help on it.

 Before resorting to the Help system for a menu item, try looking at the status bar message in the lower left of your screen. These short messages are often enough to get you started in figuring out what a command actually does. The message displays while the menu item is highlighted.

 See Help⇨Contents for a discussion of the context-sensitive Help system.

The various Access Help systems are discussed in Chapter 6 of *Access 2 For Dummies.*

Help⇨Search

Goes through the Help file looking for topics that match the words that you provide. The only problem is that you have to guess what keywords the person who wrote the Help system used to identify particular topics. Fortunately the list in the search dialog box contains all of those terms.

Just the facts

After you've opened the Search dialog box (either by selecting Help⇨Search or by clicking the Search button from within Help), you are presented with an unlabeled text box in the upper left. That's where you enter what you're looking for.

Start typing either a word or phrase that describes what you are looking for. As you type, the Help system displays the closest matching phrase. If none of the suggested phrases is quite what you need, try deleting what you've typed and using a different phrase.

When you find a phrase that seems to describe what you want, click on the Show Topics button, which will list all of the Help entries that are associated with that phrase. Look through the list for the one that seems closest and click on it. You'll find that the topics listed are generally related and that you can move between them. You can also select the Search button from any topic, and it will return you to the list that you started from.

More stuff

You can also use context-sensitive help (discussed under Help⇨Contents) or the Help⇨*Identify Command* feature to find your topic.

The various Access Help systems are discussed in Chapter 6 of *Access 2 For Dummies.*

Help⇨Technical Support

Tells you who to call and how much it costs. Actually there is a lot of very useful information hidden away in here and it's worth checking for an answer to any problem you encounter.

Just the facts

Selecting this command takes you to a special part of the Help system that describes your options in contacting technical support. Perhaps more importantly, this section also contains advice on trying to solve your problem yourself.

More stuff

 When you call technical support, they may ask you for information about your system. The easiest way to collect this information is to select the Help⇨About Microsoft Access command and click on the System Info button.

Query⇨Add Table

Includes a new table when designing a query. You need to do this task in order to ask questions based upon fields in the database or to include information from the fields in the results of the query. You use this command when you are creating a question to ask of your database.

For mouse maniacs

 Adding tables is something you do quite often for a complex query, so the Add Table button can be very useful.

Just the facts

 Select Query⇨Add Table; you are presented with a list of all of the tables within the database. Simply click on the table that you want and then click on the Add button. That's it. You can now click on the Close button and go back to designing your query.

More stuff

To select more than one table, hold down the Ctrl key while clicking on the table name. Holding down the Ctrl key adds the table to the existing group.

 The table that you are adding must already be part of the database. If it isn't, you need to use File⇨Attach Table to put the table into the database and then Query⇨Add Table to add it into the query screen. You can use Query⇨Remove Table to remove a table from the query, but it's easier to highlight the table and press Delete.

 Information on the Add Table command is in Chapter 13 of *Access 2 For Dummies*.

Query ⇨ Append

Changes the query into an *Append query,* which is a fancy way of saying that the records created by the query are added to the end of another table. The names of the fields need to match in order for Access to know where to put each item.

For mouse maniacs

Need a quick way to change the type of query to Append? Click on the Append Query button.

Just the facts

To create an Append query, you must start in the database containing the information. You then design a Select query that gets all of the records that you want to add somewhere else. Make sure that you include every field that you want to add to the other database. After you are confident that your Select query is working properly, you convert it to an Append query by returning to the Query Design screen and then using Query⇨Append. When you select Append, you are asked to provide the name of the table where the information is to be added and where that table's located (in the current database or a different database). After you've given Access that information, run the query one more time and the information that you selected is copied over to the new location.

More stuff

You don't have to run the first query using Query⇨Select to make sure that the right records are being selected, but it's a good idea. If you realize that you made a mistake, you need to go to the table where you put the new information, delete the new stuff (perhaps using a Delete query), and then go back to the where the original information is to try again. If you made a mistake the first time, then it's even more important to try a Select query the next time to make sure that you got it right.

For more information, see the entries starting with Query⇨ (such as Query⇨Select).

Chapter 12 and Chapter 13 of *Access 2 For Dummies* guide you through the basics of setting up your own queries.

Query ⇨ Crosstab

Creates a summary table of values organized by two fields in your database. In order to really use a *Crosstab query*, you need to have data that is organized into subcategories that repeat. In your datasheet, this kind of organization will be shown by one field (the first category) that repeats for each name in the second category.

For mouse maniacs

 One click of the Crosstab Query button and your query is transformed into a Crosstab query. Of course, you need to specify how to organize the summary table.

Just the facts

A Crosstab query takes the values from a single field and organizes them into a grid based upon the values in two other fields. To get a better idea, take a look at a sample of the results of a typical Crosstab query. This example totals up the number of plastic parts in the various building sets scattered around the floor.

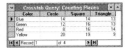

In some ways, Crosstab queries are the easiest to set up because they can only involve three fields — one for the row heading, one for the column heading, and one for the actual values in the table.

When setting up a Crosstab query, first select Query ⇨ Crosstab. Next, add the three fields that you want to use to create your table. After you've inserted your three fields, you use the Crosstab row to indicate which one is the Row Heading and which one is the Column heading. Both of these headings are marked as Group By in the Total row. Finally, you need to mark the field that you want summarized as Value in the Crosstab row and indicate the type of calculation you want in the Total row. The most common choices are Count (how many are in each category), Sum (find the total for each category), and Avg (find the average of the values in each category). The query screen used for the preceding sample looks as follows:

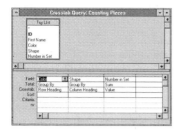

More stuff

For an even easier approach, select a new query and use the Wizard to help you design your Crosstab query.

For more information, see the entries starting with Query⇨ (such as Query⇨Select).

Chapter 12 and Chapter 13 of *Access 2 For Dummies* guide you through the basics of setting up your own queries.

Query⇨Delete

Seeks outs and destroys records that match the criteria in the query. It's generally a good idea to run a Select query first to make sure that you're actually getting what you want as your results (see Query⇨Select). Otherwise, you may delete much more than you intended.

For mouse maniacs

Be careful: clicking the Delete Query button changes your query to a Delete query, which can be quite dangerous.

Just the facts

The first step in using this command is to create a column in the query design representing the table containing the records to be deleted. To do this task, find the entry on the field list with the table name followed by an asterisk (*) and drag it onto the query design. This field should be marked as "From" in the Delete row. Next, design the selection rules for picking which records you are going to delete. Each of these fields should contain "Where" in the Delete row. Finally, select Query⇨Delete. When you run the query, instead of listing the match records, Access will delete them.

More stuff

If you are deleting from a table that is linked to another table, be aware that you may end up deleting records from the second table as well. The situation is caused by an option called Cascade Delete, which is set as part of the definition of the relationship. When this option is selected, if you delete a record in the primary table, then all of the related records in the second table also go away.

For more information, see the entries starting with Query⇨ (such as Query⇨Select).

Chapter 12 and Chapter 13 of *Access 2 For Dummies* guide you through the basics of setting up your own queries.

Query⇨Join Tables

The first in an amazing new series of non-commands from Microsoft. All this command does is show you a reminder about how to join two tables.

Just the facts

Select this command to see a dialog box that (briefly) tells you how to join two tables together. The best shortcut is to remember how to do this task in the first place.

More stuff

You need to use Query⇨Add Table to put the tables into the query.

Chapter 13 of *Access 2 For Dummies* talks about creating queries that use more than one table.

Query⇨Make Table

Takes the results of the query and uses them to create a new table. You can then use the new table for reports or as the basis for another database.

For mouse maniacs

The only danger in using the Make Table Query button is that using this type of query can create unnecessary tables.

Just the facts

Although you can actually design your criteria before or after changing the query type, it's generally best to first set your criteria, check the query as a Select query, convert it to a Make Table query, and then run it again. (This query is based upon the same screen as the one used by Query➪Select.)

When you select Make Table, a dialog box asks for a name for the new table and where to put it. You can either add the table to the current database or any other existing database on your system. Most often you'll want to add the table to another database, except perhaps when you are changing the structure of your existing database. You can use a Make Table query to rearrange the fields that are in the different tables.

More stuff

Because this query type just changes what happens with the result of the query, I suggest (very strongly) that you first design your query to select the records that you want (with Query➪Select), make sure that those records are indeed the ones that you want to put into a new table, and then run the query a second time with Query➪Make Table selected.

For more information, see the entries starting with Query➪ (such as Query➪Select). You use Query➪Append to add information to an existing table.

Chapter 12 and Chapter 13 of *Access 2 For Dummies* guide you through the basics of setting up your own queries.

Query➪Parameters

Uses the design of a query that you've set up previously (generally a Select query) but lets you change the rules used for selecting the records. This command is useful for a query that you run quite often.

Just the facts

Using Query➪Parameters is almost, but not quite, programming. It's certainly too complex for a shortcut. First, design the query that you want to automate and make sure that it works properly with the types of values that you will normally use. Next, replace the information on the Criteria row (or rows) with the message that you want Access to use when asking you for the criteria rules. Put each phrase inside of square brackets so that Access will recognize it as a message. You can replace some or all of your criteria information. Whatever you don't put in square brackets will be used each time you run the query.

The final steps require that you copy all of these messages into the Query Parameters dialog box. Although you can peek at the query screen behind the dialog box, it's easier if you have a written list. So, as you work, you may want to write down each of the phrases (be sure to spell everything correctly and include capitals and punctuation). Next, selecting Query⇨Parameters reveals the heart of creating a parameter query, the Query Parameters dialog box.

On each row, enter one of your messages. The order that you list them will be the order that Access asks for the information. You should also go to the Data Type column and let Access know what type of data to expect for each message. Close the box and you now have a Parameter query. When you run the query, Access will use your phrases as the messages for dialog boxes that ask you for the criteria information.

More stuff

A Parameter query automates some other type of query, so you need to know how to set up the original. For more information, see the entries starting with Query⇨ (such as Query⇨Select).

Query⇨Remove Table

Throws a table out of the query screen. You only need to remove a table if the screen is getting too crowded.

For keyboard krazies

You don't really delete the table; you just throw it out of the query.

Just the facts

Just select the table that you want to move off of the query screen and either select the command or press the Delete key.

More stuff

 To add a table in, use Query⇨Add Table. (Wow! A command name that makes sense. How original.)

Query⇨Run

Takes a query and makes it go out and do its job. All of the other query commands are used to set up the query. This command actually activates the query. You use this command when you are creating a question to ask of your database.

For mouse maniacs

 The Run Query button gets that old query up and running.

Just the facts

Select Query⇨Run to actually make your query work. That's all there is to it.

More stuff

 You can preview the results of a Delete query by selecting View⇨Datasheet. Selecting Query⇨Run actually goes ahead and gets rid of the records.

 There are two other Run commands — one on the Macro menu and one on the Object submenu. Both of these commands are beyond the scope of this Quick Reference.

 Chapter 12 of *Access 2 For Dummies* tells you how to set up a Select query and run it.

Query⇨Select

Creates a listing of the information that matches your criteria. You use this command whenever you just want an answer to a question. This command is most often combined with a report format to produce a printed document.

For mouse maniacs

   The Select Query button changes a query to a simple select query.

Just the facts

You use the basic Select query to choose which records are displayed in what Microsoft calls a *dynaset*. Translating for normal folk, a query just shows you a part of your data rather than a whole table. The main thing that you must understand is that the changes you make to the query results are made to the actual data. When you go back to the table, you'll see the same changes.

The query screen has two main parts. The upper portion is used to display any tables that are involved in the query, and the lower portion is used to create the rules involved in picking which records to display. A typical query screen looks like this:

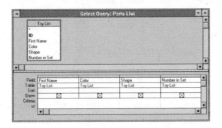

When you first open a query screen, you won't see the row labeled Table. To add this row to your query screen, simply select View⇨Table Names. The first step in creating a query is getting the field lists for the tables that you want to work with. To do that, use Query⇨Add Table. Each of the tables will appear in the upper portion of the screen with any relationships shown by lines between the field lists.

Next, you need to decide which fields you are going to use in your query. A field is included for one of two purposes: so that it is included in the final results, or so that it can be used as part of the rules for picking records. (It's also possible to use the same field for both.)

Find the names of the fields that you want to use in the field list and drag them onto the lower portion of the screen. You should add the fields in the order that you want them to appear in the final results. Don't worry about where you put the fields that are just going to be used as part of the rules, but make sure that you include them. If you want to include all of the fields from a table, drag the field name that is made up by the table name followed by an asterisk (*). If you want to rearrange the columns in the lower portion, simply click at the top of the column to select it and then drag it to the new location. For each field that you want to have in the query results, make sure that there is a check mark in the Show Row check box. If you don't want the field to appear, make sure that the Show Row check box is empty.

If you want, you can use the Sort row to indicate how the records should be organized. In a query, Access sorts from left to right, so make sure that your most important category is the first one (reading left to right) with a sorting instruction.

Finally, select Query ⇨ Run to see the results. Because you haven't included any rules at this point, every record in your database will be displayed in the query results. Notice that only the fields you marked in the Show row are included, and they're organized in the columns indicated on the query — not necessarily the way they are in the actual table.

If you want to limit which records are displayed, you need to insert rules on the Criteria row. One way to insert rules is to use the Expression Builder (discussed under the entry for, you guessed it, Expression Builder). Many of the rules that you want to use are fairly simple and can be entered from memory. If you want to only find records that match a value, just enter the value on the Criteria row under the proper field name. If you want to match several values, enter each on its own line. The example shown in the following figure matches Shapes with either "Circles" or "Triangles."

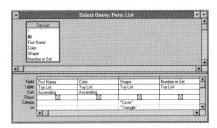

If you want to compare values, you need to use the comparison symbols. These are = (equals), > (greater than), and < (less than). If you want to find all of the toys where there are four or more in each set, you would enter ">=4" in the Number in Set field. You don't put any quotation marks, just the instructions.

If you want to get all of the records with values that are between two numbers (or two dates, or even alphabetically between two words), you simply insert "Between ? and ?" (use values in place of the two question marks). The following example finds all the sets with between four and seven pieces.

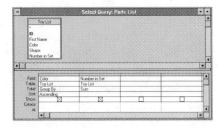

That's all there is to creating queries that just produce dynasets (or, in English, just pick out some of the records based upon your rule). You should know that if you enter rules for more than one field on the same line, only those records that match all of the rules on the line will be displayed. If you enter rules on separate lines, records that match any of the rules will be included in the query result. That's it for a basic Select query, but not all that you can do with the Select query screen.

If you think about it, you may want to actually do something with the numbers contained in your records. To do that, you need to add the Total row by using View➪Totals. When you click in the Total row, you can use a drop-down list of options. If you just want to summarize the values across all the records in the database, enter the appropriate action (Sum, Avg, or whatever) in the Total row for each field that you are including in the query. It's that simple.

There are only three options on the list that aren't actions and only two that deserve special mention. (Expression is much too complex for such a little book!)

The more important of the two, Group By, is used when you want Access to summarize information based upon values in one of the fields. In the following example, the toys are grouped by color, and the total number of toys are displayed.

If you want to limit which records are included for a Group By field, simply enter the rule that you want to use on the Criteria row.

If you enter a rule for a field that has an action (such as Sum) in the Total row, Access will select out those records that meet the rule *after* performing the calculation. If you are totaling the number of pieces in all of the sets and grouping by color, Access will find a total for each color and then compare it against your rule (for example, greater than four). So you will have a record for each color where there are more than four pieces in that color.

If you want the records to be selected before the calculation, you need to add a second column for the field and use Where in the Criteria row. This addition tells Access to only perform the action (Sum) for those records *where* the rule is true. In that case, Access will look at each set of pieces, throw out any with four or fewer pieces, group the rest by color, and total up the number of pieces for each color. Your total will be less this way because some of the sets (those with four or less pieces) aren't included.

More stuff

 If you want the column in the query results to have a name other than the field name (or the one provided by Access for calculations), just type the name that you want to use before the name of the field in the Field row. You need to separate your column name and the real field name with a colon (:).

 You can also use the wildcards discussed with Edit⇨Find when entering text in the Criteria row. Access will add the word "Like" before the query to remind you that you are using wildcards.

 A Select query forms the basis for both the Delete and Make Table queries. It's a good idea to first run your query as a Select query to make sure that it picks out the right information; then change the query type and run it again.

 You may want to convert queries that you often run with only minor changes into Parameter queries (see Query⇨Parameters). For more information on queries in general, see the commands that begin with Query⇨ (such as Query⇨Append).

 Chapter 12 and Chapter 13 of *Access 2 For Dummies* guide you through the basics of setting up your own queries. Chapter 12 tells you quite a bit about setting up a Select query.

Query⇨SQL Specific

Contains all of the submenu commands for controlling how Access interacts with a SQL database when passing queries and information. If you didn't understand any of the previous sentence, don't worry because this information probably doesn't matter to you. This command is only used when the actual database exists on another computer and you are using the database over a network.

Just the facts

Selecting Query⇨SQL Specific gives you a list of commands that are used to create queries for SQL databases. You only use these queries if an outside program that understands SQL is managing the information that you are using. Explaining how SQL works is way beyond the scope of this book, more than my contract is worth, and, probably more than I could do without a better computer and more coffee.

More stuff

If you want to see what's really going on with your query when you work with an SQL database, you can use View⇨SQL.

Query⇨Update

Finds records that match your criteria and replaces the current information based on the rules that you provide. You have to be careful that you are very clear in telling Access what to do. Remember, like small children, computers do exactly what you tell them — particularly when you didn't mean what you said.

For mouse maniacs

Click once on the Update Query button and your query is immediately turned into the Update variety.

Just the facts

To work with an Update query, you first design a Select query to pick out the records that need to be changed. When you select Query⇨Update, you lose the Sort, Show, and Totals rows, and a new row is added to the query screen called, appropriately enough, Update. Because an Update query is used to change the information in your database rather than display it, you don't need the other three rows.

You use the Update row to tell Access what rule to use when replacing the original information. If you just want to replace one value with another, you simply enter the new value. The field (or fields) that you're updating and the field (or fields) that you're using to select the records don't have to be the same. In the following example, there was a rather messy accident at the play school and now all of the circles are sort of a dingy gray.

You can use a calculation in the Update row based upon any field that is associated with that record, which generally means any field in the same table. But with certain types of relationships, you can even use fields that are in separate tables. To set up more complex updating rules, it's often easier to use the Expression Builder (discussed under the Expression Builder entry).

After you've entered the updating information, simply run the query (using Query⇨Run), and Access will let you know how many records will be changed. This pause is your last chance to decide whether you're making a horrible mistake and should get out by clicking Cancel. If you click OK, Access will go ahead and change the records.

More stuff

It's often a good idea to run your query first by using Query⇨Select to see which records are going to be included. You can then change the query type (using Query⇨Update) and add in the necessary information about how to update the field.

For more information on queries, see the other commands that begin with Query⇨ (such as Query⇨Append).

Chapter 12 and Chapter 13 of *Access 2 For Dummies* guide you through the basics of setting up your own queries. Update queries are discussed in detail in Chapter 13.

Records⇨Allow Editing

Controls whether or not you can make changes to the contents of your database. This command is sort of silly because either the database is yours and you want to make changes (so don't bother with this command), or the database was designed by someone else, and if they didn't want you to make changes, they probably set it up so that you couldn't change this command.

Just the facts

There's no shortcut for this command because you set it separately for each object in a database. You will probably never need to use it unless you are designing your own databases.

If you try to change the information in your database and can't, select Records⇨Allow Editing. Access will place a check mark next to the command, which means that it's OK to edit the information. If for some reason, you are worried about making accidental changes to your information, select the command and make sure that there is no check mark next to it in the Records menu.

More stuff

 If you want to add new records, you can use either Records⇨Data Entry or Records⇨Go To and move to a New record. The commands on the Security menu (see the entries under Security⇨) provide a means for controlling access to Access.

 Chapter 5 of *Access 2 For Dummies* talks about how to edit information after it's in your database.

Records⇨Apply Filter/Sort

Limits which records you are viewing and organizes them based upon the rules set in the Filter/Sort screen.

For mouse maniacs

 The Apply Filter/Sort button actually uses the filter and sort combination that you created.

Just the facts

You have to have first set up a filter by using Records⇨ Edit Filter/Sort. This command takes the rules in the filter and applies them to the current table or form, displaying only those records that match the rules that you provided and sorting those records in the order that you requested.

More stuff

 To set the filter, you need to use Records⇨Edit Filter/Sort. To see all the records again, use Records⇨Show All Records.

Records⇨Data Entry

Takes you to a new, blank record and displays only the records that you have added during this session.

Just the facts

There's no particular shortcut for this command and, in most cases, it's easier to use the Records⇨Go To⇨New command (or its button). But if you want to have a datasheet containing nothing but your new records, simply select Records⇨Data Entry and your wish will be granted.

More stuff

If you want to change existing information in a database, you may need to use Records⇨Allow Editing. (Often, especially if you designed the database yourself, the records are stored so that you can edit them without having to do anything special.) See View⇨Sorting and Grouping for information on sorting information within reports.

Records⇨Edit Filter/Sort

Lets you set rules for deciding which records to view and in what order to display them. Using this method is often faster than designing a query.

For mouse maniacs

After pressing the Edit Filter/Sort button, you still have to define all of the information for the filter and sort.

Just the facts

Unlike a query, a filter is based upon only the fields in the table or form that you started from, and a filter always displays all of the fields on the table or form. But other than those two restrictions, a filter works much like a basic Select query.

The easiest thing to do with a filter is to sort your data using several columns. To do this task, you need to move to the Filter/Sort screen by selecting Records⇨Edit Filter/Sort. Find the names of the fields that you want to use for the sort in the field list and drag them onto the lower portion of the screen. As with a query,

Access sorts from left to right, so make sure that your most important category is the first one (reading left to right). Next, select whether you want that field sorted in Ascending or Descending order (or not at all) by selecting the appropriate choice from the box on the Sort row. Finally, to get the sort going, select <u>R</u>ecords⇨Appl<u>y</u> Filter/Sort. If you want to limit which records are displayed, you need to insert rules on the Criteria row. As with a sort, you need to put the field names that you are going to be using into the first row (labeled *Field*).

You will need to insert the instructions that make up the rules. For a filter, the rules that you want to use are fairly simple and can be entered from memory. For more complex rules, you should use a query (see <u>Q</u>uery⇨<u>S</u>elect Query). If you want to only find records that match a value, just enter the value on the Criteria row under the proper field name. If you want to match several values, enter each on its own line.

If you want to work with comparing values, you need to use the comparison symbols: = (equals), > (greater than), and < (less than). If you want to get all of the records with values that are between two numbers (or two dates, or even alphabetically between two words), you simply insert "Between ? and ?" and use values in place of the two question marks. For more information (and an example), see <u>Q</u>uery⇨<u>S</u>elect.

More stuff

You need to use <u>R</u>ecords⇨Appl<u>y</u> Filter/Sort to actually change the records that you are viewing. Use <u>R</u>ecords⇨<u>S</u>how All Records to undo a filter. If you just want to sort your records on the information in a single field, you can use <u>R</u>ecords⇨Quick Sort instead.

You can also use a query instead of a filter to limit what you see. Chapter 12 of *Access 2 For Dummies* introduces the basics of working with queries.

<u>R</u>ecords⇨<u>G</u>o To

Moves you to a record based on its position in the database (rather than its contents). You can also use the command to move to a new record in order to add new information. When working with reports, the command takes you to the appropriate page rather than a record.

For mouse maniacs

To move to the first record, click on the First Record button, which is down at the bottom.

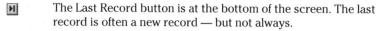

The Last Record button is at the bottom of the screen. The last record is often a new record — but not always.

This Next Record button (located at the bottom of the screen) is useful for browsing through your records. In some cases, you can also use the scroll bars to move through the records.

The Previous Record button is at the bottom of the screen. It moves you, you guessed it, to the previous record.

Record: 20 To go to a specific record, click in the Record Number box and type the record number. (It's at the bottom.) Then press Enter or Tab.

To get a new record for adding information, just click on the New button.

For keyboard krazies

To go to the FIRST record:

The first record is always number one (anywhere).

Ctrl + **↑**

This shortcut takes you to the current field for the first record (for forms).

Ctrl + **Home**

This shortcut takes you to the first field for the first record (for grid layouts).

To go to the LAST record:

Ctrl + **↓**

This shortcut takes you to the current field for the last record (for forms).

Ctrl + **End**

This shortcut takes you to the last field for the last record (for grid layouts).

To go to the NEXT record:

Use the left and right arrow to move between fields (for forms).

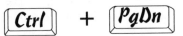

Use Tab (forward) and Shift+Tab (backward) to move between fields (for grid layouts).

To go to the PREVIOUS record:

Use the left and right arrow to move between fields (for forms).

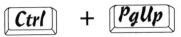

Use Tab (forward) and Shift+Tab (backward) to move between fields (for grid layouts).

To go to a SPECIFIC record:

Now just enter the record number and press enter.

Just the facts

Well, first you'd better figure out where it is you want to go. Then select the command that's most likely to get you there. You use the Previous and Next buttons to browse through your information (particularly when it's organized as a form). You use the New button (or menu command) when you're ready to add new information. Finally, there are shortcuts for moving to either the first or last record of your database.

More stuff

You can also use Records⇨Data Entry to add new records. Use Edit⇨Find to move among records based on their contents.

Chapter 5 of *Access 2 For Dummies* includes information about moving around in your database.

Records⇨*Quick Sort*

Puts the records in order based upon the current field. You have the choice of ascending (from smallest to largest) or descending (largest to smallest) order. When you are looking at a datasheet (either a table or the results of a query) or designing a table, this command is available.

For mouse maniacs

 The Sort button puts records in order based on the selected fields in A to Z order.

 The Descending Sort button puts records in order based on the selected fields in Z to A order.

Just the facts

Simply select the field that you want to use for the sort and then select whether you want the records to be sorted in ascending or descending order. You can either select from the submenu that you get when you use *Records*⇨*Quick Sort* or use the buttons on the toolbar.

More stuff

 You can actually sort on more than one column as long as the columns are side-by-side. Instead of highlighting just one column, highlight as many as you need. Access always sorts from left to right, so make sure that the most important field is the one furthest to the left.

 For more complex organizations of your data, you need to use *Records*⇨*Edit Filter/Sort* or create a query.

Records⇨*Refresh*

Makes your records feel cool and comfy. Particularly useful for those hot August days. Actually, this command is only used when you are working on a network where someone else may have changed the data while you were looking at it. Access sends out requests to everyone else on the network to make sure that your copy of the data is up-to-date.

Just the facts

If you think that someone else on the network may have changed your data while your back was turned, simply select Records⇨Refresh to get an up-to-the-minute update of the current information.

More stuff

Access does not display any new records that someone else has added while you were working with the data. To see those records, you need to requery the main database by pressing Shift+F9.

Records⇨Show All Records

Undoes any selections put in place by a filter. Try this command if you seem to be missing some records that you know existed just a minute ago.

For mouse maniacs

The Show All Records button basically undoes any filters or selections. Although the command is available, the button isn't when you are working with a query.

Just the facts

This command works under the assumption some records aren't being displayed because they don't match the rules in your filter. In order to see all of your records again, simply go ahead and select Records⇨Show All Records — one of those rare commands that does exactly what it says.

More stuff

Records⇨Show All Records works together with Records⇨Edit Filter/Sort to let you quickly control what you are looking at. You can design a filter and move back and forth between using it and seeing all your data by using Records⇨Apply Filter/Sort and Records⇨Show All Records.

You can also use a query instead of a filter to limit what you see. Chapter 12 of *Access 2 For Dummies* introduces the basics of working with queries.

Relationships⇨Add Table

Puts a table from the current database onto the layout area. You need to have the table displayed in order to create any relationships involving it. You use this command when you are changing the relationships (links) between the tables in your database. (Edit⇨Relationships opens that display.)

For mouse maniacs

 You can use the Add Table button to add tables that you then relate.

Just the facts

Selecting Relationships⇨Add Table displays the Add Table dialog box, which lists tables and queries. At the bottom of the dialog box is a set of three radio buttons: Tables, Queries, and Both. You use these to control what's shown on the list. From the list, you can select a table or query and click on the Add button. In the case of a table, Access places the selected table on the layout. If you add a query, Access adds all of the tables included in the query. When you've added all that you want, simply click on the Close button.

More stuff

 To work with all of the relationships within a database, first close all tables and then move to the Database window and open the layout screen (by using Edit⇨Relationships). Use the Add Table command to add all of the tables to the layout. To work with only those tables associated with a particular table or query, use the Add Table command and add only the table or query that you want.

 The layout that you see when you first select Edit⇨Relationships is controlled by File⇨Save Layout. If you generally work with the same tables, simply put them on the layout and then save the layout so that they're available every time you open the window.

 You may want to look at all the entries under Relationships⇨, including Relationships⇨Remove Table. Use Edit⇨Clear Layout to start over with a blank layout.

 Chapter 18 of *Access 2 For Dummies* introduces the basics of database relationships.

Relationships⇨*Create Relationship*

Gives you a message box about how to create relationships with your mouse. It's another in the new series of non-commands from Microsoft. You use this so-called command when you are changing the relationships (links) between the tables in your database.

For mouse maniacs

Use the mouse pointer to drag the field from the parent record to the field that you want to relate it to.

Just the facts

Don't bother selecting this command unless you can't remember how to use the mouse to create a relationship. All this command does is give you a message box with simple instructions. Hey, I can do that! To create a one-to-many relationship, select the field that is to be the parent end of your relationship (the one) and drag it to the field that represents the child end (the many). The parent end of the relationship is the one that represents the link to the information contained in the child file. If you are creating a one-to-one relationship where both records are required, you can drag from either field to the other. If you want to use advanced features such as Cascade Delete, you need to drag from the field in the required (parent) field to the field in the optional (child) record.

See Relationships⇨Show All for a sample of the display.

More stuff

To see any existing relationships involving a table shown on the layout, select the table and then Relationships⇨Show Direct. Any tables with a direct link to the one selected will be added to the layout. To see all of the tables that have a link back to any of the tables in the layout, select Relationships⇨Show All.

You may want to look at all the entries under Relationships⇨. After you create a relationship, the most useful command is Relationships⇨Edit Relationship. Use Edit⇨Clear Layout to just start over.

Chapter 18 of *Access 2 For Dummies* introduces the basics of database relationships.

Relationships⇨Edit Relationship

Opens the Relationships dialog box where you can set the
characteristics of the relationship. You use this command when
you are changing the relationships (links) between the tables in
your database.

For mouse maniacs

Double-click on the line representing the relationship that you
want to change.

Just the facts

To edit a relationship, you can either double-click on the line
representing the relationship or select the line by clicking once
and then selecting Relationships⇨Edit Relationship. In either
case, you end up with the Relationships dialog box:

The list at the top of this dialog box shows all of the existing
relationships between the joined tables. You can use this list to
change a relationship or create an additional relationship, but the
original relationship must be created first (see
Relationships⇨Create Relationship).

The most important option on the Relationships dialog box is
Enforce Referential Integrity. If the box next to this option is not
checked, Access doesn't check the relationship. If this box is
checked and the radio button is set to One, then the records in
the two tables must be joined in a one-to-one relationship, which
means that both fields must be set to No Duplicates. If the Enforce
Referential Integrity option is checked and the radio button is set
to Many, then the first field cannot contain duplicates, but several
records can have the same value in the second (related) table.
The various types of relationships are described under
Relationships⇨Show All.

When Enforce Referential Integrity is active, you can also choose to have Access automatically delete any related records when the associated record in the first table is deleted. You turn on this feature by checking the Cascade Delete Related Records box. Normally, you are not allowed to make changes to the value of the field that is in a relationship. Selecting Cascade Update Related Records lets you make changes that are carried across the relationship to the other table.

The Join Type button controls what happens with records that do not have a matching record in the related table (and to records in the related table that don't have a match in the first table). This setting can be changed on a query-to-query basis and is discussed under View⇨Join Properties.

More stuff

You may want to look at all the entries under Relationships⇨. See Relationships⇨Create Relationship to find out how to set up a new relationship. The command to just start over is Edit⇨Clear Layout.

Chapter 18 of *Access 2 For Dummies* introduces the basics of database relationships.

Relationships⇨Remove Table

Gets rid of the selected table. Actually, nothing happens to the table, but Access takes it out of the layout and no longer displays any relationships involving it . You use this command when you are changing the relationships (links) between the tables in your database.

For keyboard krazies

This shortcut doesn't hurt the table. It just removes it from the window.

Just the facts

To remove a table from the layout, simply select the table and then Relationships⇨Remove Table. That's it.

More stuff

You may want to look at all the entries under <u>R</u>elationships⇨, especially <u>R</u>elationships⇨<u>A</u>dd Table. To clear out everything on the layout, use <u>E</u>dit⇨Cle<u>a</u>r Layout.

Chapter 18 of *Access 2 For Dummies* introduces the basics of database relationships.

<u>R</u>elationships⇨<u>S</u>how Al<u>l</u>

Changes from working with just those relationships associated with a particular table or query to showing all of the relationships within the database. You use this command when you are changing the relationships (links) between the tables in your database.

For mouse maniacs

 Click on the Show All (Relationships) button and Access shows every relationship between the tables.

Just the facts

When you select <u>R</u>elationships⇨Show All, Access starts at the currently selected table and looks for any relationships to other tables. If it finds any, it adds those tables to the layout. It then looks for any relationships involving those tables and adds any that it finds. Access keeps looking until there are no more relationships to add to the layout. Access puts the tables onto the layout starting in the upper-left and going across the screen. In order to use the layout, you generally need to move and resize the windows so that you can see the lines representing the various relationships. After you've arranged things, you'll see something like the following:

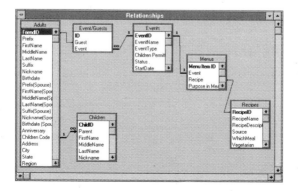

The various lines represent the existing relationships. The thinner lines (with no symbols at either end) represent relationships where there are no requirements about the relationship. In publishing, this is the relationship between a book and its author(s). A book may have one or more authors and an author may have worked on one or more books. The heavier lines with a 1 at each end indicate a relationship where each record in the first table can have one and only one match in the second table. As an example, consider a book and its cover design. Each title has only one design, and each design is associated with only one title. The third type of relationship is indicated with a line that has a 1 at one end and an infinity symbol at the other. The end with the infinity symbol marks the child or the many end of the relationship. This line indicates that there is only one record in the first table for each value, but there may be several records in the second table that share that value. For example, think of the relationship between the publisher and the book. The book can have only one publisher, but the publisher can have many books.

More stuff

To find out what you can do with the relationships while you're looking at them, see Relationships⇨Edit Relationship. For information on displaying immediate relationships, see Relationships⇨Show Direct. The command to just start over with a blank layout is Edit⇨Clear Layout.

Chapter 18 of *Access 2 For Dummies* introduces the basics of database relationships.

Relationships⇨*Show Direct*

Restricts the layout to only those tables that are directly related to the selected table — in other words, tables that are connected to the one you select with a direct line. You use this command when you are changing the relationships (links) between the tables in your database.

For mouse maniacs

When you click on the Show Direct button, Access only shows those relationships that are direct links.

Just the facts

To use this command, you must first select one of the tables on the layout. (If there's only one, it's automatically selected.) Then select Relationships⇨Show Direct to view every table that has a direct relationship to the selected table. Because relationships are represented with lines, Access will add every table that has a line between it and the selected table.

More stuff

To work with all the relationships within a database, it's best to add all of the tables to the layout and then select Relationships⇨Show All. Move the windows representing the tables around on the layout (and resize them if necessary) until you can see all of the lines clearly.

You may want to look at all the entries under Relationships⇨, especially Relationships⇨Show All. Edit⇨Clear Layout clear all of the tables off the layout.

Chapter 18 of *Access 2 For Dummies* introduces the basics of database relationships.

Security ⇨ Change Owner

Changes who has control of the objects that make up the database. The person who is the owner of the database is allowed to make any changes to the security that he or she wants. You may need to have the current owner's password in order to make any changes.

Just the facts

Be careful with this command. Changing your security settings can be dangerous. You need to be in the database containing the object(s) that you want to work with. Select Security⇨Change Owner to see the Change Owner dialog box. Use the Object Type drop-down list to select the type of object (table, form, report, and so on) that you want to reassign. Then from the Object list at the top of the screen, select the specific object(s) that you want. Next, use the New Owner box to select the name of the user or group that will be the new owner. Finally, click on the Change Owner button. Assuming that you have permission to change the owner, Access updates the Object list with the new information. When you have finished making changes, click on the Close button.

More stuff

The user or group that you intend to be the new owner must already exist to appear on the New Owner list. You must use Security⇨Groups or Security⇨Users to add to the list.

The access to each database object is controlled by the settings of Security⇨Permissions.

Security⇨Change Password

Gives you an opportunity to be creative in what you use for your password. Be careful because you need to use something that no one else will ever guess — but you'll remember after you come back from that week-long vacation in Hawaii.

Just the facts

When changing your password, you have to type your new password twice to ensure that you didn't make any mistakes the first time. To use the command, simply select Security⇨Change Password and then type your old password, press Tab, type your new password, press Tab, type your new password again, and press Enter. That's it. You're done. Now make sure that you remember what your new password is. And please don't write it on your desk calendar.

More stuff

The two commands that really control who can do what are Security⇨Permissions and Security⇨Users.

Security⇨Groups

Adds or deletes group names from the groups list. The groups list contains the names of all recognized groups. What you can do to a database may be restricted based on which groups you belong to.

Just the facts

When you select the Groups commands, you'll get a very basic dialog box listing the existing groups. To add a new group name, click on the New button. You then get a second dialog box where you need to supply both the name for the group and personal ID. The personal ID is different from a password and is used to make sure that Access can tell the groups apart no matter what their names. After you've filled in both text boxes, click on OK, and Access creates the group. To delete an existing group, select the name from the list and click on the Delete button.

More stuff

You can type the new name in the first dialog box, but doing so doesn't gain you anything as you still need to go to the New User/ Group dialog to add the personal ID.

Keep a written record of every user and group that you create, including the personal ID information. Make sure that you can tell which letters were entered as uppercase and which were lower-case. You'll need this list if you ever have to re-create the users or groups.

For information about adding users to groups, see Security⟹ Users.

Security⟹Permissions

Sets the permissions that each user (or group) has for each object within the database. This is the key command in setting up security for a database. Although permissions are easy to set, you should avoid using this feature unless you really need it.

Just the facts

When you select Security⟹Permissions, you get a single dialog box that you use to set the various permissions for each object in the database for both users and groups.

Select the object that you want to work with by using the Object Type and Object Name lists. You can only work with one type of object at a time. You must then select whether you are changing the permissions for a user or a group by selecting the appropriate radio button. The steps for a user are identical to the steps for a group.

Select the specific user from the User/Group Name list. If you selected a single object, the Permissions area in the bottom half of the dialog box now displays the current permissions for that user. Otherwise, the settings for the check boxes are grayed out.

Use the check boxes in the Permissions area to indicate what permissions the user should have. A check means that the user has that permission; a blank means that the user does not have permission for that action. When all of the permissions are set, click on the Assign button. You can then either close the dialog box (with the Close button) or change the settings for another user.

When you select Database from the Object Type list, you have two choices for types of permissions. Open/Run controls whether or not the user can even get into the database. Open Exclusive controls whether the user can open the database and lock everybody else out. If the user can open the database, he or she can automatically open any of the tables or queries within the database.

The most important permission is that of Read Design. With tables and queries, if Read Design is not checked, then the user cannot change the data in anyway. If Read Design is checked, the permissions in the second column are used to control what types of permissions are granted. Users must be given Read Data permission before they can be given Update Data permission, Insert Data permission, or Delete Data permission. A user must have Modify Design permission with queries in order to change the criteria. With tables and queries, if neither Read Design nor Modify Design is checked, then the user cannot work with that object in any way.

With forms and reports, Open/Run controls whether the user can even use the object. Read Design controls whether the user can see the design, and Modify Design controls whether the user can make changes to the design.

More stuff

To activate any security on a database, you need to use Security⇨Change Password to assign a true password to the Admin user. If there is no security in effect, you will automatically be recognized as the Admin user. After you've started security checking, you will need to provide the name and password of a user on the database's user list. You'll need to set that up before activating the security by using Security⇨Users.

It's a good idea of keep a record of the security settings by using Security⇨Print Security.

Security⇨Print Security

Produces a report listing all of the users with their group memberships and all groups with their member users.

Just the facts

After you select Security⇨Print Security, you need to choose whether you want the listing of users, of groups, or of both. After you decide, simply click on OK to preview your report. If you want an actual printed copy, select File⇨Print.

Security⇨Users

Adds new users and changes the membership of groups. Security for a database is based on the name that you use when first starting Access (your user name) and what group(s) you belong to. Security⇨Users lets the owner of a database change what groups an individual is a member of.

Just the facts

When you first select the Security⇨Users command, you see a dialog box listing all of the current users. To add a new user, simply click on the New button. You'll have to provide both a name and a personal ID. As with groups, the personal ID is different from the password and is used to help identify the user. When you click on OK, you should assign the user to the proper group(s) using the process for changing the groups that a user is in.

To change the group(s) that a user is in, you need to be in the Users dialog box. (That's the one you get from selecting Security⇨Users.) Select the user from the Name list at the top. To remove a user from a group, select the group from the Member Of list and click on the Remove button. To add a user to a group, select the group from the Available Groups list and click on the Add button. To get rid of a user, select the name from the Name list at the top and click on the Delete button.

Database administrators use the Clear Password button on those bad days when someone has forgotten the password for the database. Select the user and then click on the Clear Password button. The user is now able to get into the database without a password. After the user has gotten in, use Security⇨Change Password to assign a new password.

More stuff

For information about creating groups, see Security⇨Groups.

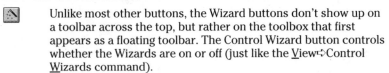

View⇨Control Wizards

Turns the Control Wizards on or off. (A check mark indicates that they are on.) The Control Wizards help you create the more complex controls on a report or form such as list boxes, combo boxes, and option groups. There is also a Control Wizard for creating control buttons that activate commands or macros as well as a Control Wizard for creating graphs. You'll find that this command is available when you are designing the layout for a report or form.

For mouse maniacs

Unlike most other buttons, the Wizard buttons don't show up on a toolbar across the top, but rather on the toolbox that first appears as a floating toolbar. The Control Wizard button controls whether the Wizards are on or off (just like the View⇨Control Wizards command).

When the Control Wizards are active, the List Box button starts up the list box Wizard.

If you are using Control Wizards, the Combo Box button starts the combo box Wizard.

The Option Group button starts up the Option Group Wizard (if the Control Wizards are active).

The Control button starts up the Control Button Wizard (if the Control Wizards are active).

Just the facts

Unlike most of the other View menu commands, selecting View⇨Control Wizards doesn't cause something to appear or disappear on your screen. In fact, when you select the View⇨Control Wizards all that happens is that the button appears to move up and down. Likewise, if you select the Control Wizard button, the check mark on the menu comes and goes.

What is really happening is that the Wizards are being turned on and off for the tools used to create list boxes (where you pick from a scrolling list), combo boxes (where you can either type a value or pick from a drop-down list), option groups (where you pick a word from a set of choices and Access converts it into a value), and control buttons (where clicking on the button actually does something). You activate the Wizards by selecting the tool to create the control that you want and then drawing the outline for the control on the design screen. The Control Wizards have to be turned on before you start drawing.

The List Box and Combo Box Wizards help you to create the association between the box and the field and to fill in the possible values that will appear on the list. You use a list box when you want the choices restricted to one of the values on the list; you use a combo box when it's possible that some new or strange value that's not on the list may be entered. To create the list without using a Wizard, you enter a simple list of values on the property sheet as the RowSource with each value separated by a semicolon (;). (The type of list is set by the RowSourceType property.)

The Wizard for option groups is quite a bit more complicated. First, you have to decide what text you want to use for each item, which of the items (if any) is the automatic (or default) choice, and what value to assign to each item. Then you decide whether the information goes into a field or is just stored for later use. Finally, you pick the style for the group box and for the buttons and give the box a name. You can have radio buttons, check boxes, or toggle buttons as the controls within the box.

The Control Button Wizard is really cool and is used primarily for more complex forms and reports. It enables you to create a button that performs an action (like moving to the next record). The Wizard presents you with a long list (organized by categories) of existing actions, and you can add your own if you know how to create macros. Like the other Wizards, simply click on the control and draw the outline on the design screen to activate the Wizard.

More stuff

If you just need a control that offers a choice between Yes and No, you can also use a single control button or check box. When the button is in the down position or the box is checked, the value is true (Yes); otherwise, it's false (No).

To use the Control Wizards, you should be viewing the toolbox that contains the tools for creating controls (View⇨Toolbox).

View⇨Datasheet

Moves you to the datasheet display. The datasheet resembles a spreadsheet in that each field is represented as a column and each record is a row. Whether you are looking at your data as a form, table, or query, or when you are designing your own tables, forms, or queries, you can use this command.

For mouse maniacs

The Datasheet button gets you to the datasheet without wasting any time.

Just the facts

Selecting this command moves you from your current view to the datasheet for the information. The datasheet (shown in the following figure) is a simple grid, much like what you see in a spreadsheet. The rows represent the records, and each column represents the fields.

More stuff

The other commands at the top of the View menu are determined by what type of object you are working with (Form or Form Design, Query or Query Design, and Report Design). To control the size of each field, see Format⇨Column Width and Format⇨Row Height.

View⇨Field List

Determines whether or not the field list is displayed when designing a report or form. (A check mark indicates that the field list is somewhere on the screen.) You'll want to display the field list whenever you are adding fields to a report or form.

For mouse maniacs

The Field List button opens and closes the field list window.

Just the facts

Just go to the menu and select the command (or click the button). When the field list is active (a check mark is beside the name on the menu), you see the field list window on the design screen. The field list, shown in the following figure, is an easy way to add fields to a report or form.

If you drag a field onto the design area, you'll end up with a text box that is linked to the field. When using the report (or form), the value in the box will be the same as the one in the field. Changing the text in the box changes the value in the field. You'll need to use the Label tool if you want text identifying what's in the box.

You can also create other types of controls that are linked to a field. First select the type of control from the toolbox and then drag the field name onto the report (or form). Instead of a text box, you'll get whatever type of control you had selected.

More stuff

If you want to be able to pick from a list of choices, make sure that the control Wizards are active (View⇨Control Wizards) and then click on either the List Box or Combo Box tool and start by drawing the border for the box on the design screen. As soon as you have placed the control, the Wizard will start and walk you through the steps of creating your list of values.

View⇨Form

Moves you to the actual form where you can view the current information. You need to move back to the form view in order to test the various features that you create while designing a form.

For mouse maniacs

Note that even though you generally are moving between designing a form and viewing a form, the View Form button is not a toggle. You must use View⇨Form Design to work with the form's design.

Just the facts

Selecting this command moves you from a form design or a form's datasheet to the actual information displayed in the form.

More stuff

To go back to designing, you use View⇨Form Design. To see the data in a grid, use View⇨Datasheet.

View⇨Form Design

Changes from just looking at a form to being able to make changes or add new features to a form. This command is available whenever you are working with a form.

For mouse maniacs

Note that even though you are generally moving between designing a form and viewing a form, the Design Form button is not a toggle. You must use View⇨Form to see the results of your work. This button is the same as the View⇨Report Design button.

Just the facts

Select the command and Access moves you to the design screen where you can make changes to your form's layout.

More stuff

You use View⇨Form to check out how well your design works. You may need to use View⇨Palette and View⇨Toolbox in order to make the form design tools available. Most of the commands for formatting the form are, not surprisingly, listed under Format⇨.

View⇨Forms

Changes the Database window so that it displays the list of available forms. For more information, see the entry for the Database window itself. (View⇨Form is a separate and different command.) Any time you're at a Database window, this command is available.

For mouse maniacs

You use the Forms button from the Database window to view existing forms or to start the process of creating a new one.

Just the facts

View⇨Forms is the Database window command for viewing the list of forms. It just changes what's shown in the Database window.

More stuff

View⇨Form is a different command that you use to move from designing to viewing an individual form.

Working with the Database window is discussed under the entry of the same name.

View⇨Grid

Shows or hides the dots that make up the design grid. (A check mark indicates that the grid is being displayed.) Turning off the display of the grid makes it easier to see what your form or report looks like, but because the grid is still there, it's easy to make changes. You'll find that this command is available when you are designing the layout for a report or form.

Just the facts

View⇨Grid is a toggle. A check mark next to the command means that the grid is being displayed, but it's easier just to look at the screen to find out. With the grid displayed, it's easier to line things up. Without the grid displayed, you can get a better idea of what your form looks like without the measles.

More stuff

See Format⇨Snap to Grid for more information about using the grid. See View⇨Ruler for information about hiding the ruler at the top of the screen.

View⇨Indexes

Opens the Indexes window, which lists the fields that are indexed. Indexing a field speeds up sorting the information in the database based upon that field and makes searching for the field faster with the Edit⇨Find command. If you are designing a table, this command is very useful.

For mouse maniacs

The View Indexes button opens the Indexes window. Imagine that.

Just the facts

View⇨Indexes is another toggle. Select it once; see the Indexes window. Select it again; hide the Indexes window.

The fastest way to set an index is to click in the field name column on a blank row and then use the drop-down list to select the field that you want as an index. (If you know the field name, you can also just type the first view letters until it appears in the box.) Use Shift+Tab to move to the Index Name column and enter text to identify the index (it can be the same as the field name). That's it.

More stuff

 A single index can be built using more than one field. Simply use a separate row for each field and use the same index name for all of them.

 To set a field as an index without the Indexes window, you need to be in Table Design mode and on the field that you want to index. Set the Indexed property (down at the bottom of the screen) to Yes (Duplicates OK) or Yes (No Duplicates).

 Each table must have one and only one special indexed field called the primary key. You set the primary key using <u>E</u>dit⇨<u>S</u>et Primary Key.

<u>V</u>iew⇨<u>J</u>oin Properties

Displays the properties of any joins (relationships) between tables in a query and lets you change the characteristics of the properties. You use this command when you are creating a question to ask of your database.

Just the facts

First, select the connecting line representing the tables' relationship in the upper part of the query window. When you select the <u>V</u>iew⇨<u>J</u>oin Properties command, you are rewarded (punished?) with the following dialog box:

Selecting among the options is a matter of deciding which of the three choices describes what you want. In the preceding figure, the names of the two tables in the database will replace "Adults" and "Children."

More stuff

You can also just double-click on the line representing the relationship to display the Join Properties dialog box.

To see more of an overview of the relationships involved in your query, you can use Edit⇨Relationships and the commands on the Relationships menu.

The basics of database relationships are discussed in Chapter 18 of *Access 2 For Dummies*.

View⇨Options

Reveals the rather ugly and needlessly complex dialog box for setting the options that control how Access really works. Fortunately, most of these options can be set for individual objects by using other commands. No matter where you are, you can get to this command.

Just the facts

After you select the View⇨Options command from the menu, you see the Options dialog box:

The list at the top lets you select the category of options that you are dealing with (in the figure, Printing). To change an option, simply click in the text box and select from the list (if one is available) or type the new value.

Many of the options set the default value (the value that will be used for a new object). The values for an existing object can be changed by using a menu command (in the case of the preceding figure, File⇨Print Setup).

Controls whether the Palette is available when designing a report or form. The Palette enables you to determine how a control looks in terms of style, color, and thickness of the lines. The Palette is a *floating toolbar,* which means that you can move it around and change its shape. (A check mark to the left of the command name indicates that the Palette is somewhere on screen.) This command is available when you are designing the layout for a report or form.

For mouse maniacs

The entire Palette is actually a toolbar controlled by the Palette button.

Just the facts

Using the View⇨Palette command is a very easy. Just select it and the Palette will appear (or, if it was already there, disappear). The Palette is the floating toolbar (the box) at the bottom of this screen:

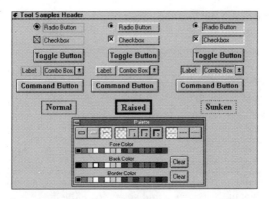

To use the Palette, you first select the control or controls that you want to change and then click on the buttons on the Palette to change the look. The first three buttons (in the upper left) set the appearance of the control. From left to right, the choices are normal, raised, and sunken. The groups of controls in the upper portion of the screen show the various controls formatted with the different appearances.

The next four buttons control the thickness of lines. The labels below the controls are all formatted with a normal appearance, but with different types of lines for the borders. The "Normal" label has a hairline border; the "Raised" label has a 3 point border (a point is 1/72 of an inch). The last three buttons control what type of line is used for the border. The choices are solid, dashed, or dotted. The third label, "Sunken," is formatted with a 1 point, dotted border.

The bottom portion of the Palette sets the colors of the various controls. For most controls, all three color bars are available — Fore Color, Back Color, and Border Color. The Fore Color is the color used for the text. In addition to the colors on the bar, both the Back Color and the Border Color have a toggle button labeled "Clear." When the Clear button is selected (in the down position), the background (or border) is transparent. It doesn't matter what color you assign to a clear background (or border) because it will not actually appear on the form or report.

More stuff

If you aren't satisfied with the colors available on the standard bar, you can use the Color Builder to design your own. First, select a control and then the control's property sheet (using View⇨Properties). Next, find the appropriate property (Fore Color, Back Color, or Border Color) from the Layout Properties list. When you select the text box for one of the color properties, the Build button appears to the right of the text box. Click on that button and then the Define Custom Colors button. You can use the right side of the screen to create your color and then click on the Add To Custom Colors button to use the color.

To format a group of controls with the same look, select all of the controls as a group before making your formatting changes. (Hold down the Shift key and click on a control to add it to the group.) If you want to set the format for a particular type of control (for example, all the radio buttons), you can use the default format. To store the format, you first format one of the controls using the Palette and menu commands and then select Format⇨Change Default. To use the format for another control of the same type, click on the control and select Format⇨Apply Default. Any new controls of that type will be created using the new default format.

View⇨Toolbox controls whether the floating toolbar that contains all of the tools for creating controls is displayed or not. For more information about formatting the text on a control, see Format⇨*Text for Controls*.

For an example of using the Palette to change the look of a control, see Chapter 14 of *Access 2 For Dummies*.

View▷Properties

Shows you the properties sheet for the selected object. Many of the most powerful features of Access are controlled by settings on the properties sheets. The fact that many of the settings have drop-down lists where you can select an option makes using these features fairly straightforward.

For mouse maniacs

 Click once on the Properties button and the Access real estate agent will give you a tour of the object's properties.

Just the facts

Select an object (or control) and then View▷Properties to reveal the property sheet for that object (or control). The property sheet controls both the look and behavior of the object (or control). You can either view all of the properties in a single list or use the drop-down list at the top to select more organized categories such as Data Properties or Layout Properties.

To change a property's value, simply move to the white text box and either select a value from the list (if available) or type in the new value. In many cases, the properties can also be set by a menu command. In such cases, the property name and the menu command name will be similar.

More stuff

 You need to use Edit▷Select Form or Edit▷Select Report before using View▷Properties in order to see the underlying property sheet for a form or report.

 For an example of using a control's properties, see Chapter 14 of *Access 2 For Dummies.*

View▷Queries

Changes the Database window so that it displays the list of available queries. For more information, see the entry for the Database window itself. (Note that View▷Query Design is a separate command.) Any time you're at a Database window, this command is available.

For mouse maniacs

You use the Queries button from the Database window to view existing queries or to start the process of creating a new one. An even better shortcut for creating a new query is to use the New Query button.

Just the facts

Just select the command (or the tab) to change what objects are being listed in the Database window.

You can simply double-click on an action query (indicated with an exclamation mark at the start of the name) to start the query.

More stuff

Working with the Database window is discussed under the entry of the same name.

View⇨Query Design

Moves you to the query design screen where you can construct questions. The settings in the query screen determine what you will see when you are looking at the datasheet. Whenever you are working with a query, you'll be able to use this command.

For mouse maniacs

Yep. The Query Design button is the same as the one for designing other objects.

Just the facts

View⇨Query Design takes you to the query design screen (as shown in the following figure) where you can set the rules for your query.

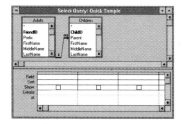

Some of the information on the query screen changes based upon your selections on the View and Query menus. For example, to see the Table Names and Totals rows, the commands of the same name must have a check mark on the View menu.

More stuff

Setting up criteria is discussed under the Query⟹Select entry. You can use the commands on the Query menu to change the type of query and some of its characteristics (see the entries under Query⟹).

Chapter 12 of *Access 2 For Dummies* gives an introduction on how queries work.

View⟹Report Design

Not an actual Access command, but I needed an excuse to talk about the Report Design button. The Report Design button takes you to the report design screen where you can make changes in the structure and format of your report. You have to be designing a report to use this command.

For mouse maniacs

You have to use the Report Design button to return directly to the report design after switching to viewing your report. Your only other option is to go back via the Database window.

Just the facts

Clicking on the Report Design button takes you to a design screen very similar to the one available when designing forms.

More stuff

While still working on your design, it's better to use the preview buttons to get an idea of what the finished product will look like. Both Print Preview and Sample Preview return you to the design screen when you are finished.

There is no View⟹Report command. Instead, you use File⟹Sample Preview or File⟹Print Preview to see what your report will look like.

Chapter 17 of *Access 2 For Dummies* introduces the basics of working with report design; Chapter 19 goes into more detail about designing your own.

View⇨Reports

Changes the Database window so that it displays the list of available reports. For more information, see the entry for the Database window itself. (View⇨Report Design is a separate command.) Any time you're at a Database window, this command is available.

For mouse maniacs

Click on the Reports button to see what reports have been saved or to begin creating a new report (although using the New Report button is easier).

Just the facts

Just select this command to change the list on the Database window to the reports that you have stored. You also use this command as the first step in creating a new report via the Database window.

More stuff

Working with the Database window is discussed under the Database Window entry.

View⇨Ruler

Shows or hides the ruler across the top of the design screen. Generally, the ruler is very useful for seeing where things are positioned on the report; however, hiding it does free up a little bit more room for displaying the report. A check mark next to the command indicates that the ruler is being displayed. You'll find that this command is available when you are designing the layout for a report or form.

Just the facts

All you need to do is select the command to make the ruler disappear. Select the command again and the ruler comes back.

More stuff

The dots across your screen are not measles, but rather the points of the *grid*. For more information about the grid, see View⇨Grid.

View⇨Sorting and Grouping

Opens the Sorting and Grouping dialog box, which is where you tell Access how to organize the records for a report. The sorting instructions are only used when producing an actual report. You have to be designing a report to use this command.

For mouse maniacs

 The Sorting and Grouping button opens the Sorting and Grouping dialog box.

Just the facts

Selecting View⇨Sorting and Grouping displays the dialog box that you use to organize the records for a report. The dialog box, shown in the following figure, is fairly simple to use when you understand that Access reads the list from top to bottom.

The first thing you should do is decide which fields you are going to use to organize the data. There are two ways in which a field can be used. The first is for sorting the information. The order of the fields in the list determines how Access sorts the records. Always put the most important field for sorting first in the list. By most important, I mean the one that you want the entire list organized by. The other fields will only be used if the information in the first field matches. (For example, in a normal alphabetical sorting of names, you only look at the first name when the last name is the same.)

The second use for a field in a report is for grouping. To understand grouping, you first have to understand how reports are created. Each report has what is called a *detail line*. The detail line is the section that is printed for each and every record in the report. In order to make a report useful, you want to be able to do calculations that summarize the values for groups of records. In order to do that, you have to create what is called a *group header* or a *group footer*. These grouping sections are only printed when the value for the associated group field changes. (A header appears before the detail line and a footer appears after the detail line.) The grouping sections usually contain organizational information (such as printing the current value of the field in the header) and a calculated field that summarizes the values in the field for the records in the group (usually in the footer). For example, you would put the name of the group in the header and the total for one of the fields in the footer.

To create a section for a field, change Group Header, Group Footer, or both to Yes in the Sorting and Grouping dialog box. A single field can have both a header and a footer. Again, the order on the list is crucial. The first group is the broadest category. Any other groupings will be within that group. For example, if you were creating a report on the populations of various areas, you would first group on State, then on County, and finally on City. This organization gives you separate totals for each city within the county, subtotals for each county within the state, and an overall total for the state.

More stuff

A field used for grouping must also be sorted.

If you just want to sort the information on your screen, you can use either Records⇨Quick Sort or Records⇨Edit Filter/Sort. To see how your report is going to look, use either File⇨Print Preview or File⇨Sample Preview.

View⇨SQL

Shows you the Structure Query Language (SQL) instructions that you wrote when you created a query for a networked database. Access uses these instructions to communicate with the real database, which is hidden away on another computer. Don't worry about what it all means. If your query didn't work, you probably aren't going to fix it by staring at these statements. Instead, you should try re-creating your query.

For mouse maniacs

The SQL button reveals more than you probably wanted to know about how Access actually works with networked databases.

Just the facts

Selecting View⇨SQL causes a separate window to open that contains the query expressed in Structured Query Language (SQL). If you know SQL, this feature is great. If you don't, you should probably leave it alone.

More stuff

If the SQL instructions are hard to read, you can use Ctrl+Enter to set each line apart.

When designing a query, use the Query⇨SQL Specific submenu to control how Access and the other databases communicate.

View⇨Subform Datasheet

Shows you the datasheet associated with information on a *subform*. A subform is a section of a form that displays information from a second table based upon a relationship between the two tables.

Just the facts

The standard View⇨Datasheet command opens the main datasheet associated with a form. Select View⇨Subform Datasheet to open the datasheet associated with a subform. Because a form can have more than one subform, you should select the subform before selecting the command.

More stuff

The format used for the subform is stored as an independent form. To view that form, open it from the Database window.

Chapter 18 of *Access 2 For Dummies* discusses the topic of relationships between tables.

View⇨Table Design

Takes you to the table design screen, which lists each field on an individual row and the properties for the current field at the bottom. The table design screen is used to change the actual structure of your database. This command is available whenever you are working with a table.

For mouse maniacs

Like the other Design buttons (for Forms, Reports, and what not), the Table Design button is not a toggle. To get back to viewing the table, you have to use the Datasheet button.

Just the facts

Select this command to move to the screen used for describing the fields in a table. Be careful when working with this screen because it defines the structure that supports your table. If you delete a field, all of the information in that field is lost.

More stuff

Chapter 3 of *Access 2 For Dummies* introduces the table design screen.

View⇨*Table Names*

Changes the field names in the query window so that they also include the name of the table that they come from. (A check mark means that the table name is displayed as part of the field name.) You use this command when you are creating a question to ask of your database.

For mouse maniacs

The Table Names button is a toggle. Click once; the list appears. Click again; it disappears.

Just the facts

Select View⇨Table Names and your query screen grows a new row labeled Tables that contains the name of the table for each field. To get rid of the table names, select the command again.

More stuff

View⇨Field List is particularly useful when you are creating forms or reports.

View⇨*Table Properties*

Displays a table's properties sheet. The properties sheet includes a blank for inserting a description of the table. It's a good idea to fill in this blank so that you have a record of what you were thinking when you designed the table. This command is very useful when designing tables.

For mouse maniacs

 Click on the Table Properties button and the Access real estate agent reveals the properties of the table that you are currently working with.

Just the facts

Unlike most other objects, the properties for each field in a table are displayed at the bottom of the design screen. To see the properties for a field, first move to that field. Because of this setup, the only other property sheet available is the one for the entire table. That's why instead of the <u>V</u>iew⇨<u>P</u>roperties command, you have the <u>V</u>iew⇨Table <u>P</u>roperties command. Just select it to view the table's property sheet.

More stuff

 It's rare that setting a validation rule for an entire table is the best solution. In most circumstances, you'll just want to set rules field by field.

 To get to the underlying properties sheet for a form or report, you have to first use either <u>E</u>dit⇨Select Fo<u>r</u>m or <u>E</u>dit⇨Select <u>R</u>eport. Only one or the other will be available depending on what you are designing.

View⇨*Tables*

Changes the Database window so that it is displaying the list of available forms. For more information, see the entry for the Database window itself. Any time you're at a Database window, this command is available.

For mouse maniacs

 The Tables button from Database window shows you what tables are in the current database or lets you start the process of creating a new table (although using the <u>N</u>ew Table button is faster).

Just the facts

Select <u>V</u>iew⇨<u>T</u>ables to have the Database window display all of the tables in the current database. That's all there is to it.

More stuff

Working with the Database window is discussed under the entry of the same name. Generally, you use View⇨Datasheet to see the contents of a database table when you are already working with a report or form based on that table.

View⇨Toolbars

Displays a dialog box for controlling which toolbar is being displayed (something you don't usually want to change) and three toolbar features: color buttons, large buttons, and ToolTips. This dialog box is also the starting point for changing a toolbar or creating a new one. No matter where you are, you can get to this command.

Just the facts

Select View⇨Toolbars and you get the following dialog box:

There are a number of things that you can do with this dialog box. Along the bottom are three check boxes that control various toolbar features. Two of these, Large Buttons and Color Buttons, change the look of the toolbar. The third, Show ToolTips, controls whether the ToolTips feature is active. When ToolTips is active (the box is checked), holding the mouse pointer over a button causes a small text box to appear containing the button name. This feature is very useful when you are trying to learn the various toolbar shortcuts. Turning off ToolTips may improve performance slightly when selecting buttons from a toolbar.

Probably the most powerful feature of this dialog box is the capability to add new buttons representing commands to a toolbar. First, select the toolbar that you want to change from the Toolbars list. (The section, "A Toolbar Tour," identifies the buttons and format for most of the standard Access toolbars.) Two blank toolbars, Utility 1 and Utility 2, are included for you to build your own. In addition, you can create a new toolbar by clicking on the New button and typing a name. After you've decided which toolbar you want to change, click on the Customize button.

You are then presented with a second dialog box that lists categories of actions within Access (such as File or Form Design) plus any objects in the current database. You now need to find the button representing the command that you want to add. A word of warning: not all commands have a button in the standard list. To find the button, select the category most likely to contain the command that you want to add and check out the buttons. When you position the pointer over a button, the description for that button appears at the bottom of the dialog box. To actually add the button, drag it from the dialog box onto the toolbar. You should try to place it where you want it the first time, but if you miss, you can rearrange the buttons on the toolbar by dragging them to their new positions. To delete a button from a toolbar, drag the button onto the Customize dialog box.

More stuff

 To change between an anchored toolbar (one along the top (below the menus) or along any side) and a floating toolbar, double-click on the toolbar's background. To anchor a toolbar to a side, drag the floating toolbar towards the side until the outline changes to the proper, narrower shape and then release.

View⇨Toolbox

Controls whether or not you can work with the tools used to create controls when designing a form or report. The toolbox is pretty central to designing forms or reports, so the only reason you might hide it is to show a bit more of the form or report. A check mark to the left of the command name indicates that the toolbox is displayed somewhere on the screen. This command is available when you are designing the layout for a report or form.

For mouse maniacs

 The Toolbox button controls whether or not you see the toolbox while designing a report or form.

Just the facts

Using View⇨Toolbox is easy. If the toolbox is hidden, when you select the command the toolbox will appear. If the toolbox is somewhere on the screen, there's a check mark to the left of the

command on the menu and the button appears depressed. Select
the button when the toolbox is already showing and the button
pops up, the check mark disappears, and the toolbox disappears.

Of course, using the tools on the toolbox is a bit more complex.
Basically, to create a control, you select the appropriate tool and
draw its boundaries on the form or report by dragging with the
mouse. It's generally easiest to start in the upper-left corner and
drag to the lower-right. After it's part of the design, you use the
mouse to adjust the position, and you use the various other
commands to format its appearance. You keep adding controls
and changing the layout and formatting until you have what you
want. Then switch views to find out what it really looks like. The
following figure shows all of the ToolTip names for the buttons on
the toolbox.

Select Objects		Text Box
Label		
Option Group		Toggle Button
Option Button		Check Box
Combo Box		List Box
Graph		Subform/Subreport
Object Frame		Bound Object Frame
Line		Rectangle
Page Break		Command Button
Control Wizards		Tool Lock

More stuff

 The behavior of each control is managed by the control's
property sheet. To see the property sheet, select the control and
then View⇨Properties. The Palette, the Format⇨*Text for Controls*
commands, and the mouse set the layout properties.

 The tools that you use when designing reports or forms are
controlled by View⇨Palette. A number of menu settings change
either how the tools work or the look of the design; you may want
to check out Format⇨Snap to Grid, View⇨Grid, and
Format⇨Align.

 For a quick introduction to using the toolbox, see Chapter 19 of
Access 2 For Dummies.

View⇨Totals

Controls whether or not you even have the *option* of controlling
the way groups are summarized in the query results. When
View⇨Totals is active (it has a check mark), there is a Totals line

on the query screen. You can then select how the values in the field are grouped (summed, counted, and averaged are just three common examples). In the results of your query, you'll just see a variant of the field names and the "total." If you are averaging the results of the cost field, what you get is a field heading of "TotalOfAverage" and a single row containing the average value. You use this command when you are creating a question to ask of your database.

For mouse maniacs

 The Totals button toggles between showing and hiding the totals line on the query screen (down for display; up for hide).

Just the facts

Selecting View⇨Totals adds the total row to the query screen. (Unless it's already there, in which case selecting View⇨Totals makes the row disappear.) When the Totals row is displayed, you can select an option from the drop-down list to control how the information in the query results is summarized.

The Group By option is used to control how the data is grouped. If none of the fields contain a Group By entry on the Totals row, then all of the records in the query are summarized into a single group. If only one field contains a Group By entry, then a summary value is produced for each distinct value in that field. When two or more fields contain a By Group entry, a value is created for each possible combination. For example, if you are grouping both by color (Red or Blue) and shape (Circle or Square), then there are four combinations (Red Circle, Red Square, Blue Circle, and Blue Square).

Most of the remaining options are used to indicate what type of calculation should be used to create the summary value. Options include Sum, Avg, Max, Min, and Count. In addition, there are two statistical functions, Var (variance) and StDev (standard deviation), and also two options that are based on record position: First and Last.

If you want more than one type of summary calculation, you must repeat the field in your query and use a separate column for each calculation.

More stuff

 For more information on using the Totals row, see Query⇨Select.

Window⇨Arrange Icons

Arranges icons representing the various opened objects along the bottom of the Access screen. Each icon represents a separate object (such as a query, report, or form).

Just the facts

As soon as you select the command, any windows that have been reduced to icons will line up neatly in a row at the bottom.

More stuff

In order for this command to do any good, you must have already minimized at least some of the windows that you were working with. To organize your windows, use either Window⇨Cascade or Window⇨Tile.

Window⇨Cascade

Organizes all of the open windows so that each title bar is displayed. Because a picture is worth a thousand words (although not by my contract), see "Just the facts" for an idea of what the cascade looks like.

Just the facts

As soon as you select the command, your windows are re-arranged (as shown in the following figure).

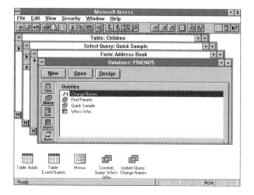

These windows are organized in a cascading fashion. No matter which one I pick, a little bit of each window will still be showing. Just click on the visible part of the window to make it active and move it to the top of the pile.

More stuff

You can also organize windows so that you can see a bit of the contents of each by using Window⇨Tile. If you have objects that are reduced to icons, you can use Window⇨Arrange Icons to make them line up neatly.

Window⇨Database: Name

Moves you to the Database window for the database represented by *Name*. For more information about what you can do when you're at the Database window, see its entry.

For mouse maniacs

The Database Window button takes you to the Database window associated with the object that you are working with.

For keyboard krazies

If you don't have an F11 key, you can use Alt+F1.

Just the facts

Just select the database from the Window menu or use one of the shortcuts. The Database window is your organizer for all of the objects within your database and therefore central to working with your entire database. Because you can only have one database open at a time, there is only one Database window available.

More stuff

For information about actually working with the Database window, see its entry.

Window⇨Hide

Removes the window representing the current object from the screen and also from the list of open objects on the Window menu. The object remains open and can be referenced from other objects. This command is most useful when you are designing a database for someone else to use, and you don't want them to know how you did it.

Just the facts

Select this command and the current window seems to disappear. The information from the window is still available (and in fact can be used by other objects such as macros), but you can't see it. This feature helps keep your work area less cluttered.

More stuff

If you start hiding things, you'd better know how to bring them back with Window⇨Unhide.

Window⇨List of open objects

Lets you quickly move between all of the open objects. This method is generally much faster than going back to the Database window and selecting objects from there. If part of a window is visible, you can just click directly on it. The list represented by this entry appears at the bottom of the Window menu.

Just the facts

To move to one of the objects on the list, simply select the object's name from the menu. This feature is most useful when you have maximized your windows and can therefore only see one at a time. Otherwise, if part of the window that you want to work with is showing, you can just click on that part of the window to make it active and move it to the front.

More stuff

See Window⇨Tile and Window⇨Cascade for information about organizing your windows.

Window⇨Size to Fit Form

Adjusts the size of the current form window to match the borders of the form, or, if the form is larger than a single screen, maximizes the window. You use this command primarily to make the screen look neater, which, in itself, is a good thing (I'm a fussy Virgo). When you are looking at a form, this command is there to make the window fit the form.

Just the facts

When you are viewing a form, go the to the Window menu and select this command to adjust the boundaries of the window to match those of the form (if the form is smaller than a single screen). If the form is larger than a single screen, the window is adjusted to the maximum possible size.

More stuff

Window⇨Size to Fit Form will not work when you have the windows maximized.

See Window⇨Cascade and Window⇨Tile for information about organizing the windows that you are currently using.

Window⇨Tile

Organizes all of the open windows so that a bit of each window is displayed.

Just the facts

Just select this command to arrange the windows into separate tiles on the screen. The number of windows open determines the arrangement. The following example shows four windows:

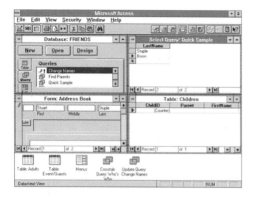

If you have any windows reduced to icons at the bottom of the screen, the tiling will allow room to view the icons (as in the example). If not, the entire screen will be used and there will be no space at the bottom for icons.

More stuff

You can also organize windows so that you can see the title bar of each by using Window⇨Cascade. If you have objects that are reduced to icons, you can use Window⇨Arrange Icons to make them line up neatly.

Window⇨Unhide

Displays a list of all hidden windows. If this command is available, then the current database has at least one hidden object window.

Just the facts

Selecting Window⇨Unhide gives you a list of all hidden windows. (If this command is not available, then you don't have any windows hidden.) You can only "unhide" (who taught these people English?) a single window at a time. To bring the window back, either double-click on the window name or click once and then click on the OK button. To bring back another window, you'll need to select Window⇨Unhide again and go through the same steps.

More stuff

See Window⇨Hide for information about how the object window got hidden in the first place.

Part II

A Toolbar Tour

One of the reasons for using a quick reference is to learn faster ways to work with the covered program. (That's why we call it "quick.") In Access, there are two major shortcuts for most commands. The first is the right-button menu. If you're looking for a way to speed up tasks, check to see if the command that you need is available by pressing your right mouse button. If so, just select it and off you go. The second shortcut, and the focus of this section of the book, is the toolbar.

This Toolbar Tour presents each button on each toolbar. These buttons are labeled with their actual ToolTip names (which you can see in Access if you hold your pointer over the buttons), the names of the commands, and brief descriptions of what the commands do. With this kind of help, you can learn the commands on the toolbars without having to resort to trial-and-error. By the way, if the ToolTips don't appear when you hold the mouse pointer over a button, see the entry for View➪Toolbar in the Command Reference section for information about turning ToolTips on.

Database Toolbar

This toolbar appears whenever you are at the Database window.

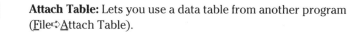

 **New Database:** Creates a new database (File➪New Database).

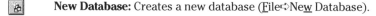 **Open Database:** Opens an existing database (File➪Open Database).

 **Attach Table:** Lets you use a data table from another program (File➪Attach Table).

Print: Prints the object selected in the Database window (File⇨Print).

Print Preview: Previews the object selected in the Database window (File⇨Print Preview).

Code: Lets you view the code associated with an object.

Cut: Removes the selected object and places it on the Clipboard (Edit⇨Cut).

Copy: Copies the selected object and puts it on the Clipboard (Edit⇨Copy).

Paste: Places the contents of the Clipboard into the Database window (Edit⇨Paste).

Relationships: Opens the layout view of the relationships between tables (Edit⇨Relationships).

Import: Starts the process of importing objects from another database (File⇨Import).

Export: Makes a copy of the selected object(s) for use in another program (File⇨Export).

Merge It: Activates the Mail Merge Wizard (File⇨Output To (Microsoft Word)).

Analyze It with MS Excel: Copies the data into a separate file for use with Microsoft Excel (File⇨Output To (Microsoft Excel)).

New Query: Starts a new query either with or without using the Query Wizard (File⇨New (Query)).

New Form: Starts a new form either with or without using the Form Wizard (File⇨New (Form)).

New Report: Starts a new report either with or without using the Report Wizard (File⇨New Report).

Database Window: Takes you to the Database window for the current database — which is where you are if you're using this toolbar (Window⇨Database: *Name*).

AutoForm: Starts the Form Wizard (File⇨New (Form)).

AutoReport: Starts the Report Wizard (File⇨New (Report)).

Undo: Reverses the last action (Edit⇨Undo).

Cue Cards: Opens the Cue Cards for step-by-step instruction in Access (Help➪Cue Cards).

Help: Changes the pointer so that clicking on a command or button opens Help to that topic (Help➪*Identify Command).*

Filter/Sort Toolbar

This toolbar is available when you are designing a filter.

Save: Saves the filter as a query screen (File➪Save As Query).

Apply Filter/Sort: Selects records based upon the filter's rules and optionally sorts them (Records➪Apply Filter/Sort).

Database Window: Takes you to the Database window for the current database (Window➪Database: *Name).*

Undo: Reverses the last action (Edit➪Undo).

Cue Cards: Opens the Cue Cards for step-by-step instruction in Access (Help➪Cue Cards).

Help: Changes the pointer so that clicking on a command or button opens Help to that topic (Help➪*Identify Command).*

Form Design Toolbar

This toolbar is available when you are designing a form.

Design View: Design must be selected to view the toolbar (View➪Form Design).

Form View: Changes to viewing the form being designed (View➪Form).

Datasheet: Changes to viewing the datasheet for the information in the form (View➪Datasheet).

Save: Saves the form under its current name. If not named, you are given a chance to name it (File⇨Save).

Print Preview: Previews the object selected in the Database window (File⇨Print Preview).

Properties: Displays the property sheet for the selected control or section (View⇨Properties).

Field List: Controls whether or not the field list is being displayed (View⇨Field List).

Code: Displays the code associated with the selected control.

Toolbox: Controls whether or not the toolbox is displayed (View⇨Toolbox).

Palette: Controls whether or not the Palette is displayed (View⇨Palette).

Font Name: Controls the font used for the selected control(s) (Format*Í**Text for Controls*).

Font Size: Controls the size of the font for the selected control(s) (Format⇨*Text for Controls*).

Bold: Toggles between bold and plain text for the selected control(s) (Format⇨*Text for Controls*).

Italic: Toggles between italic and plain text for the selected control(s) (Format⇨*Text for Controls*).

Left-Align Text: Aligns the text in the selected control(s) to the left edge (Format⇨*Text for Controls*).

Center-Align Text: Centers the text in the selected control(s) (Format⇨*Text for Controls*).

Right-Align Text: Aligns the text in the selected control(s) to the right edge (Format⇨*Text for Controls*).

Database Window: Takes you to the Database window for the current database (Window⇨Database: *Name*).

Undo: Reverses the last action (Edit⇨Undo).

Cue Cards: Opens the Cue Cards for step-by-step instruction in Access (Help⇨Cue Cards).

Help: Changes the pointer so that clicking on a command or button opens Help to that topic (Help⇨*Identify Command*).

Form View Toolbar

This toolbar is available when you are viewing information in a form.

Design View: Changes to the design view for the current form (View⇨Form Design).

Form View: Must be selected to view the toolbar (View⇨Form).

Datasheet View: Changes to viewing the datasheet for the information in the form (View⇨Datasheet).

Print: Prints the information as formatted by the form (File⇨Print).

Print Preview: Previews the form with the information from the selected records (File⇨Print Preview).

New: Moves to a blank form where you can enter a new record (Records⇨Go To (New)).

Cut: Places the selected text, field(s), or record(s) on the Clipboard (Edit⇨Cut).

Copy: Copies the selected text, field(s), or record(s) and puts it on the Clipboard (Edit⇨Copy).

Paste: Pastes the contents of the Clipboard onto the current record (Edit⇨Paste).

Find: Opens the Find dialog box to search for matching text (Edit⇨Find).

Sort Ascending: Sorts the records into ascending order on the selected field(s) (Records⇨Quick Sort (Ascending)).

Sort Descending: Sorts the records into descending order on the selected field(s) (Records⇨Quick Sort (Descending)).

Edit Filter/Sort: Opens the filter design screen (Records⇨Edit Filter/Sort).

Apply Filter/Sort: Selects records based upon the filter's rules and optionally sorts them (Records⇨Apply Filter/Sort).

Show All Records: Ignores any filtering rules and displays all of the records (Records⇨Show All Records).

Database Window: Takes you to the Database window for the current database (Window⇨Database: *Name*).

Undo Current Field/Record: Reverses any changes made to the current record (Edit⇨Undo Current Field/Record).

Undo: Reverses the last action (Edit⌐Undo).

Cue Cards: Opens the Cue Cards for step-by-step instruction in Access (Help⇨Cue Cards).

Help: Changes the pointer so that clicking on a command or button opens Help to that topic (Help⇨*Identify Command*).

Print Preview Toolbar

This toolbar is displayed when you are previewing (with either Print Preview or Sample Preview).

Close Window: Closes the preview and returns you to the screen from which you started (File⇨Print Preview).

Print: Prints the object selected in the Database window (File⇨Print).

Print Setup: Opens the Print Setup dialog box (File⇨Print Setup).

Zoom: Controls whether your see the entire page or the text as it will be printed (File⇨Print Preview).

Publish It with MS Word: Creates a file formatted as it appears on screen for use with Microsoft Word (File⇨Output To (Microsoft Word)).

Analyze It with MS Excel: Creates a file containing the data for use with Microsoft Excel (File⇨Output To (Microsoft Excel)).

Mail It: Sends the file via an electronic mail system (File⇨Send).

Database Window: Takes you to the Database window for the current database (Window⇨Database: *Name*).

Cue Cards: Opens the Cue Cards for step-by-step instruction in Access (Help⇨Cue Cards).

Help: Changes the pointer so that clicking on a command or button opens Help to that topic (Help⇨*Identify Command*).

Query Datasheet Toolbar

This toolbar appears when you are looking at the results of a query.

Design View: Switches to the query screen where you create the actual query (View⇨Query Design).

SQL View: Displays the query rules as SQL instructions. The toolbar is also displayed with this selection, but most of the buttons are inactive (View⇨SQL).

Datasheet View: Must be selected to see the toolbar (View⇨Datasheet).

Print: Prints the information as formatted by the form (File⇨Print).

Print Preview: Previews the form with the information from the selected records (File⇨Print Preview).

New: Moves to a blank form where you can enter a new record (Records⇨Go To (New)).

Cut: Places the selected text, field(s), or record(s) on the Clipboard (Edit⇨Cut).

Copy: Copies the selected text, field(s), or record(s) and puts it on the Clipboard (Edit⇨Copy).

Paste: Pastes the contents of the Clipboard onto the current record (Edit⇨Paste).

Find: Opens the Find dialog box to search for matching text (Edit⇨Find).

New Query: Starts a new query either with or without using the Query Wizard (File⇨New (Query)).

New Form: Starts a new form either with or without using the Form Wizard (File⇨New (Form)).

New Report: Starts a new report either with or without using the Report Wizard (File➪New (Report)).

Database Window: Takes you to the Database window for the current database (Window➪Database: *Name*).

AutoForm: Starts the Form Wizard (File➪New (Form)).

AutoReport: Starts the Report Wizard (File➪New (Report)).

Undo Current Field/Record: Reverses any changes made to the current record (Edit➪Undo Current Field/Record).

Undo: Reverses the last action (Edit➪Undo).

Cue Cards: Opens the Cue Cards for step-by-step instruction in Access (Help➪Cue Cards).

Help: Changes the pointer so that clicking on a command or button opens Help to that topic (Help➪*Identify Command*).

Query Design Toolbar

This toolbar appears when you are designing a new query.

Design View: Must be selected to view the toolbar (View➪Query Design).

SQL View: Displays the query rules as SQL instructions. The toolbar is also displayed with this selection, but most of the buttons are inactive (View➪SQL).

Datasheet View: Changes to viewing the datasheet containing the information for the query (View➪Datasheet).

Save: Saves a copy of the query. If it's not already named, you are prompted to name it (File➪Save).

Run: Runs the query and switches to the datasheet to view the query results (Query➪Run).

Properties: Displays the property sheet for the selected control (View➪Properties).

Add Table: Displays a list of tables which you can use to add tables to the query (Query⇨Add Table).

Totals: Adds the Totals line to the query screen (View⇨Totals).

Table Names: Adds the table names (in the Table line) to the query screen (View⇨Table Names).

Select Query: Makes the current query a Select query (Query⇨Select).

Crosstab Query: Adds the Crosstab row and makes the current query a Crosstab query (Query⇨Crosstab).

Make-Table Query: Makes the current query a Make Table query (Query⇨Make Table).

Update Query: Adds the Update row and makes the current query an Update query (Query⇨Update).

Append Query: Makes the current query an Append query (Query⇨Append).

Delete Query: Makes the current query a Delete query (Query⇨Delete).

New Query: Starts a new query either with or without using the Query Wizard (File⇨New (Query)).

New Form: Starts a new form either with or without using the Form Wizard (File⇨New (Form)).

New Report: Starts a new report either with or without using the Report Wizard (File⇨New (Report)).

Database Window: Takes you to the Database window for the current database (Window⇨Database: *Name*).

Build: Opens the Expression Builder window.

Undo: Reverses the last action (Edit⇨Undo).

Cue Cards: Opens the Cue Cards for step-by-step instruction in Access (Help⇨Cue Cards).

Help: Changes the pointer so that clicking on a command or button opens Help to that topic (Help⇨*Identify Command*).

Relationships Toolbar

This toolbar appears when you are viewing the layout of the relationships among the tables in the database.

Save: Makes the current layout what you will see whenever you open the Relationships window (File➪Save Layout).

Add Table: Displays a list of the tables and queries in the database which can be used to add them to the layout (Relationships➪Add Table).

Show Direct Relationships: Adds any tables that are directly related (by a single connection) to the ones on the layout (Relationships➪Show Direct).

Show All Relationships: Adds any tables that are related to the ones on the layout no matter how many links are between the current tables and the ones added (Relationships➪Show All).

Database Window: Takes you to the Database window for the current database (Window➪Database: *Name*).

Cue Cards: Opens the Cue Cards for step-by-step instruction in Access (Help➪Cue Cards).

Help: Changes the pointer so that clicking on a command or button opens Help to that topic (Help➪*Identify Command*).

Report Design Toolbar

This toolbar appears when you are designing a report.

Design View: Must be selected to view the toolbar.

Print Preview: Previews the report with actual data (File➪Print Preview).

Sample Preview: Previews the report with only a portion of the data (File➪Sample Preview).

Save: Saves the report's design. If the report has not been named, you are prompted to supply one (File⇨Save).

Sorting and Grouping: Opens the dialog box used to control the organization of records in the report (View⇨Sorting and Grouping).

Properties: Displays the property sheet for the selected control (View⇨Properties).

Field List: Controls whether or not the field list is being displayed (View⇨Field List).

Code: Displays the code associated with the selected control.

Toolbox: Controls whether or not the toolbox is displayed (View⇨Toolbox).

Palette: Controls whether or not the Palette is displayed (View⇨Palette).

Font Name: Controls the font used for the selected control(s) (Format⇨*Text for Controls*).

Font Size: Controls the size of the font for the selected control(s) (Format⇨*Text for Controls*).

Bold: Toggles between bold and plain text for the selected control(s) (Format⇨*Text for Controls*).

Italic: Toggles between italic and plain text for the selected control(s) (Format⇨*Text for Controls*).

Left-Align Text: Aligns the text in the selected control(s) to the left edge (Format⇨*Text for Controls*).

Center-Align Text: Centers the text in the selected control(s) (Format⇨*Text for Controls*).

Right-Align Text: Aligns the text in the selected control(s) to the right edge (Format⇨*Text for Controls*).

Database Window: Takes you to the Database window for the current database (Window⇨Database: *Name*).

Undo: Reverses the last action (Edit⇨Undo).

Cue Cards: Opens the Cue Cards for step-by-step instruction in Access (Help⇨Cue Cards).

Help: Changes the pointer so that clicking on a command or button opens Help to that topic (Help⇨*Identify Command*).

Table Datasheet Toolbar

This toolbar appears when you are looking at a table's data.

Design View: Switches you to the table design where you can change the table's structure (<u>V</u>iew⇨Table <u>D</u>esign).

Datasheet View: Must be selected to view the toolbar (<u>V</u>iew⇨Data<u>s</u>heet).

Print: Prints the datasheet (<u>F</u>ile⇨<u>P</u>rint).

Print Preview: Previews the formatted datasheet (<u>F</u>ile⇨Print Pre<u>v</u>iew).

New: Moves you to a blank line where you can add a new record (<u>R</u>ecords⇨<u>G</u>o To (Ne<u>w</u>)).

Cut: Places the selected text, field(s), or record(s) on the Clipboard (<u>E</u>dit⇨Cu<u>t</u>).

Copy: Copies the selected text, field(s), or record(s) and puts it on the Clipboard (<u>E</u>dit⇨<u>C</u>opy).

Paste: Pastes the contents of the Clipboard onto the current record (<u>E</u>dit⇨<u>P</u>aste).

Find: Opens the Find dialog box to search for matching text (<u>E</u>dit⇨<u>F</u>ind).

Sort Ascending: Sorts the records into ascending order on the selected field(s) (<u>R</u>ecords⇨Quick Sort (<u>A</u>scending)).

Sort Descending: Sorts the records into descending order on the selected field(s) (<u>R</u>ecords⇨Quick Sort (<u>D</u>escending)).

Edit Filter/Sort: Opens the filter design screen (<u>R</u>ecords⇨Edit <u>F</u>ilter/Sort).

Apply Filter/Sort: Selects records based upon the filter's rules and optionally sorts them (<u>R</u>ecords⇨Appl<u>y</u> Filter/Sort).

Show All Records: Ignores any filtering rules and displays all of the records (<u>R</u>ecords⇨<u>S</u>how All Records).

New Query: Starts a new query either with or without using the Query Wizard (<u>F</u>ile⇨Ne<u>w</u> (Query)).

New Form: Starts a new form either with or without using the Form Wizard (File⇨New (Form)).

New Report: Starts a new report either with or without using the Report Wizard (File⇨New (Report)).

Database Window: Takes you to the Database window for the current database (Window⇨Database: *Name*).

AutoForm: Starts the Form Wizard (File⇨New (Form)).

AutoReport: Starts the Report Wizard (File⇨New (Report)).

Undo Current Field/Record: Reverses any changes made to the current record (Edit⇨Undo Current Field/Record).

Undo: Reverses the last action (Edit⇨Undo).

Cue Cards: Opens the Cue Cards for step-by-step instruction in Access (Help⇨Cue Cards).

Help: Changes the pointer so that clicking on a command or button opens Help to that topic (Help⇨*Identify Command*).

Table Design Toolbar

This toolbar appears when you are designing or changing the structure of a table.

Design View: Must be selected to view the toolbar (View⇨Table Design).

Datasheet View: Displays the datasheet representing the table (View⇨Datasheet).

Save: Saves the table definition. If you have not yet provided a name, you are prompted for one (File⇨Save).

Properties: Displays the property sheet for the table (View⇨Table Properties).

Indexes: Displays the list of indexed fields in the table (View⇨Indexes).

Set Primary Key: Makes the current field the primary key (Edit⇨Set Primary Key).

Insert Row: Inserts a new, blank row before the current row (Edit⇨Insert Row).

Delete Row: Removes the current row (Edit⇨Delete Row).

New Query: Starts a new query either with or without using the Query Wizard (File⇨New (Query)).

New Form: Starts a new form either with or without using the Form Wizard (File⇨New (Form)).

New Report: Starts a new report either with or without using the Report Wizard (File⇨New (Report)).

Database Window: Takes you to the Database window for the current database (Window⇨Database: *Name*).

Build: Opens the Table Wizard. Note that the small buttons in the field properties section open the Expression Builder (File⇨New (Table)).

Undo: Reverses the last action (Edit⇨Undo).

Cue Cards: Opens the Cue Cards for step-by-step instruction in Access (Help⇨Cue Cards).

Help: Changes the pointer so that clicking on a command or button opens Help to that topic (Help⇨*Identify Command*).

builder

Well, if it were a person, it would be someone who makes things (generally houses). In Access, it's a dialog box used to make things (generally formulas). You get to a builder by either clicking on the Build button (the one with three dots on it) or by selecting Build from the right-button shortcut menu. The most common builder is the Expression Builder. In fact, that one's so important that there's an entry for it in the command reference itself. Other builders include the Field Builder, the Query Builder and the Color Builder. The Field Builder takes you to a screen from the Table Wizard that lets you pick from a list of possible fields. To get to the Field Builder, you must be in a row on the table design screen. The Query Builder is used to build select queries for use with forms or reports; it is pretty much the same as the query screen itself (see Query⇨Select). You get to the Query Builder by going to the RecordSource property on the property sheet for the report or form. The Color Builder is available for any of the color properties for any control on a form or report; it lets you pick colors.

check box

A choice in a dialog box or on a form represented by a little square box that can be switched On (it has a check) or Off (it's empty). In forms, check boxes are often used for fields that have Yes or No choices. According to the way Windows normally works, unlike radio buttons, each check box is independent.

Clipboard

A special storage place within Windows that can hold just about anything. Unfortunately, it can only hold one thing, so you need to keep track of what's in it. You put things into the Clipboard by using Edit⇨Cut or Edit⇨Copy. You get things out of the Clipboard by using Edit⇨Paste.

control

An item on a form that you add using the toolbox (see

View⇨Toolbox). Typical controls include those that hold information from a field, check boxes, radio buttons, graphs, and pictures. Each control has its own property sheet that controls how it looks and what (if anything) it does.

control button

A special type of control on your form (or report) that looks like a button with either text or an icon. When you click such a button, it does something. Typical control buttons include go to next form, go to previous form, print, and change the query.

data

Well, to tell you the truth, I use it to mean stuff that you put into your database. Computer Science instructors who are reading from their textbooks will tell you that data is the collection of facts before it's been organized, and information is what you get after you organize data. If you print an attractive, organized report listing all of the stuff in your database, that's information. If you drop the report down the stairs and the pages get all messed up, it's back to being data.

database structure

The term that database professionals (who get paid lots of money) use to describe the whole enchilada of information about the type or size of your fields, the organization of the fields within tables, and the relationships among tables. If you use this term a lot, you may get a raise.

Database window

The organizer for an Access database. Every database has a Database window and every object within the database is listed in the Database window. For more information, see the entry for Database window in the command reference.

datasheet

This is the most boring view of your data; it looks a lot like a spreadsheet. A datasheet lists all of the records as rows and all of the fields as columns, so you can see a great deal of data on your screen when its organized in this way.

data type

The fancy term for how you tell Access what type of information can be put into a field. You can also use the data type to control how Access treats the information after it's in the field. The most common data types are *text* (which can hold just about anything) and *number* (which can hold any number). Two data types that let you automatically format the information are *Currency* (money) and *Date/Time* (along with money, the one thing I'm always running out of). You can also have *Yes/No* fields (which can only have the values "Yes" or "No") and *Counter* fields (which Access fills in for you by counting the records). Whenever possible, use Yes/No instead of text — it makes Access work faster. You use the *Memo* data type when you have a lot of text that you want to store, and you promise, absolutely swear, that you'll never try to sort on that field (because you can't). The last type of data is an *OLE object,* which has its own glossary entry.

A special subtype of the number data type is *integer,* which can hold only a whole number. It's useful for talking about things that can't be divided. Don't you hate it when someone says that the average family has 2.3 children? Children should be counted in integers — you have either 2 or 3, never something in between. You set the type of number on the property sheet shown at the bottom of the table design screen.

embed

When you're talking about Windows, it means to put something created by another program (usually either a picture or a recording) into a program that can hold it, but not change it. Embedding is a part of OLE (see that entry for more info). An embedded object doesn't exist anywhere outside of the file that you are working with, but it requires a separate program to change it.

field

A big grassy area where people go for picnics and to play. Also, a category of information in a database (but not for playing). A field is the container that holds the stuff that you put into your database. The "Last Name" field can contain anyone's last name. Actually, you could probably put anything you want into the field, but because it's named "Last Name," people are going to assume that what's in this field really is the last name of someone. The only way to control what's in a field is by restricting the contents to a *data type* (see that entry for more info) or by using a *validation rule* (something that's way beyond the scope of this reference). When you're looking at a datasheet, a field is a single column containing information.

field name

The name used for referring to a field. What's inside the field doesn't really have to match the field name. When you're looking at your data in a datasheet, a field name is the text in the gray box at the top of the column.

field type

See data type. Many people also include the field size, in addition to the data type, as part of the field type.

floating toolbar

A toolbar whose shape you can adjust and whose position on-screen you can change. Most toolbars are *anchored,* which means that they are stretched along one edge of the window. To turn an anchored toolbar into a floating toolbar, just drag it away from the edge. To anchor a floating toolbar, drag it near the edge of the window. When the toolbar stretches to the length of the edge, release the mouse button and the toolbar will anchor to the window.

link

Used when you want to put a copy of something into your database that actually exists as a separate file. For more information, see the entry for OLE.

object

Something in your database that can be displayed within its own window. Tables, forms, reports, and queries are all examples of database objects.

OLE

Something a bullfighter yells. In Windows, it stands for *Object Linking and Embedding* and refers to a technique for combining things created in different programs. When it works, it's really cool. When it doesn't, it's a disaster. Imagine that your computer has a program for creating animation complete with soundtrack. Now, you decide that it would be neat to put little samples of that animation (including the nifty sounds) into your database or even a word processing document. Well, neither your word processor nor your database has the tools necessary for playing back the animation and sounds. Even worse, you may want to be able to edit the recording even after you put it into your database. So you have to have a way of putting the recording in other documents while allowing your animation

and sound programs to manage it. That's OLE! It enables you to put the recording into your document (as an OLE object), and it keeps track of the program that should be used to play back or change the recording. With OLE, you can choose between embedding the object (so that it only exists within the database) or linking it (which means that it also exists as a file on your computer).

OLE object

Any type of information inside of a document that is being managed by a second program. Examples include sounds placed inside your word processor document or your database, images created and managed by a separate graphics program, and even entire word processing documents inside of a field in your database.

Palette

A floating toolbar that is used to control the look of control on forms and reports. With the Palette, you can pick the color and style for each control. For more information on using the Palette, see View➪Palette in the command reference.

properties

The settings that control how something looks or acts. The size of letters used for text is a property of that text.

property sheet

The list of properties for an object or control. Everything

within Access has a property
sheet. In fact, the dialog box that
appears when you select
View⇨Options is sort of a
property sheet for Access. For
controls and fields, just click on
the item and select
View⇨Properties to see the
property sheet. To see the
property sheet for a form or
report, you have to use
Edit⇨Select Form or Edit⇨Select
Report first. With tables, the
command on the View menu
becomes Table Properties.

query

A question that you ask your
database. In Access, a simple
question that returns information can be either a Select query
(see Query⇨Select) or a filter
(see Records⇨Edit Filter/Sort).
Access also lets you create
action queries that make
changes to your data. You can
use a query to delete records
based upon your selection rule
(see Query⇨Delete), make
changes to your data (see
Query⇨Update), create a new
table (see Query⇨Make Table),
or add new records to an
existing table (see
Query⇨Append). Finally, you
can use a query to summarize
the information in your database
into a table based upon two of
the fields (categories). This task
is called a Crosstab query (see
Query⇨Crosstab).

radio button

A radio button is used to set an
entry as On (the center of the
button is dark) or Off (the center
of the button is cleared). Unlike
check boxes which are used for

Yes/No fields, radio buttons are
used for selecting from a group
of options where only one of the
options at a time can be on.
Although you can make radio
buttons work for Yes/No fields,
this setup often confuses people
who are used to the way
Windows normally works.

record

A round piece of vinyl used to
record music prior to the
introduction of CDs. In a
database, a record is all of the
related information about one
person or thing (depending
upon how your database is
organized). A record has one
entry for each field within the
database. When you're looking
at a datasheet, a record is the
information contained within a
single row.

table structure

The arrangement of fields
(including their *data type* and
size) within a table.

toggle button

A control in Access that has two
settings: up (or Off) and down
(or On). A toggle button, like a
check box, can be used with
Yes/No fields. If you want a
button that actually performs an
action, you need to use a *control
button* (see the glossary entry or
View⇨Toolbox).

toolbox

This floating toolbar contains all
of the tools used to create
controls for a form or report.

Wizard

A magical Microsoft tool that guides you through creating complex objects within your database. Each Wizard consists of a series of dialog boxes in which you select the options that you want for the final product. Most of the Wizards appear when you try creating a new object such as a table, form, report, or query (see File⇨New). There are also special Wizards for creating certain types of controls (see View⇨Control Wizards) and graphs (just use the Graph control in the toolbox). You can also use a special Wizard to create documents using Microsoft Word's mail merge. That Wizard is on the Database window toolbar (see File⇨Output To).

Index

• A •

Access
  closing down, 42
  copyright information, 75
  exiting, 38
  setting options, 119
actions, reversing last, 31–32, 142–144,
  148–149, 151, 153–154
Add Table button
  Query Design toolbar, 149
  Relationships toolbar, 150
Add Table command, 1
Add Table dialog box, 101
Add-in Manager, 37
add-ins
  Add-in Manager, 37
  Attachment Manager, 36
  Database Documentor, 36
  Import Database, 36
  Menu Builder, 36
Analyze It with MS Excel button
  Database toolbar, 142
  Print Preview toolbar, 146
anchored toolbar, 132, 157
Append queries, 81, 149
Append Query button
  Query Design toolbar, 149
Apply Filter/Sort button
  Filter/Sort toolbar, 143
  Form View toolbar, 145
  Table Datasheet toolbar, 152
asterisk (*) wildcard, 15
Attach dialog box, 37
Attach Table button
  Database toolbar, 141
AutoForm button, 47
  Database toolbar, 142
  Query Datasheet toolbar, 148
  Table Datasheet toolbar, 153
AutoReport button, 48
  Database toolbar, 142
  Query Datasheet toolbar, 148
  Table Datasheet toolbar, 153

• B •

Bold button
  Form Design toolbar, 144
  Report Design toolbar, 151
bold text, 144, 151
Build button, 155
  Query Design toolbar, 149
  Table Design toolbar, 154
builder, 155
buttons, 1
  ToolTip names, 141

• C •

Center-Align Text button
  Form Design toolbar, 144
  Report Design toolbar, 151
Change Owner dialog box, 107
check boxes, 155
Clipboard, 155
  copying data to, 7–9
  copying object to, 142
  copying text, fields, or records to, 145
    147, 152
  inserting as new record, 22–23
  moving objects to, 142
  pasting contents into record, 145, 147, 152
  pasting from, 8, 21–22
  placing contents in Database window, 142
  placing text, fields, or records, 145, 147, 152
Close (Ctrl+W) shortcut keys 38
Close Window button
  Print Preview toolbar, 146
Code button
  Database toolbar, 142
  Form Design toolbar, 144
  Report Design toolbar, 151
color, 121
Color Builder, 121, 155
Column Width dialog box
  Best Fit button, 64
columns
  freezing on-screen, 66
  hiding, 67
  inserting into query design, 16
  resizing, 64–65
  selecting to display, 70–71
  unfreezing, 74
Combo Box Wizards, 112–113
Command Reference, 3–140
context-sensitive help, 76
control buttons, 156
Control Buttons Wizard, 112–113
Control Wizards, 112–113
controls, 155–156
  aligning, 61–62
  bold text, 144, 151
  centered text, 144, 151
  displaying code, 144, 151
  displaying property sheet, 148
  fonts, 144, 151
  formatting group, 121
  formatting text, 72–73
  horizontal spacing, 68
  italic text, 144, 151
  left-aligned text, 144, 151
  modifying to default settings, 62–63
  moving to alignment grid, 72
  moving to top layer, 63
  positioning, 68

IDG BOOKS WORLDWIDE REGISTRATION CARD

RETURN THIS REGISTRATION CARD FOR FREE CATALOG

Title of this book: Access 2 For Dummies Quick Reference

My overall rating of this book: ❑ Very good [1] ❑ Good [2] ❑ Satisfactory [3] ❑ Fair [4] ❑ Poor [5]

How I first heard about this book:
❑ Found in bookstore; name: [6] _____ ❑ Book review: [7]
❑ Advertisement: [8] _____ ❑ Catalog: [9]
❑ Word of mouth; heard about book from friend, co-worker, etc.: [10] ❑ Other: [11]

What I liked most about this book:
_____
_____

What I would change, add, delete, etc., in future editions of this book:
_____
_____

Other comments:
_____
_____

Number of computer books I purchase in a year: ❑ 1 [12] ❑ 2-5 [13] ❑ 6-10 [14] ❑ More than 10 [15]

I would characterize my computer skills as: ❑ Beginner [16] ❑ Intermediate [17] ❑ Advanced [18]
❑ Professional [19]

I use ❑ DOS [20] ❑ Windows [21] ❑ OS/2 [22] ❑ Unix [23] ❑ Macintosh [24] ❑ Other: [25]_____
(please specify)

I would be interested in new books on the following subjects:
(please check all that apply, and use the spaces provided to identify specific software)

❑ Word processing: [26] _____ | ❑ Spreadsheets: [27]
❑ Data bases: [28] | ❑ Desktop publishing: [29]
❑ File Utilities: [30] | ❑ Money management: [31]
❑ Networking: [32] | ❑ Programming languages: [33]
❑ Other: [34]

I use a PC at (please check all that apply): ❑ home [35] ❑ work [36] ❑ school [37]
❑ other: [38] _____

The disks I prefer to use are ❑ 5.25 [39] ❑ 3.5 [40] ❑ other: [41]_____

I have a CD ROM: ❑ yes [42] ❑ no [43]

I plan to buy or upgrade computer hardware this year: ❑ yes [44] ❑ no [45]

I plan to buy or upgrade computer software this year: ❑ yes [46] ❑ no [47]

Name: _____ Business title: [48] _____
Type of Business: [49]
Address (❑ home [50] ❑ work [51]/Company name: _____
Street/Suite#
City [52]/State [53]/Zipcode [54]:_____ Country [55]

IDG BOOKS

❑ **I liked this book!**
You may quote me by name in future IDG Books Worldwide promotional materials.

My daytime phone number is _____

THE WORLD OF
COMPUTER
KNOWLEDGE

YES!
Please keep me informed about IDG's World
of Computer Knowledge. Send me the latest
IDG Books catalog.